GAME CHANGER

HOW EDUCATION, TECHNOLOGY AND CLIMATE ACTION
CHANGE THE WORLD

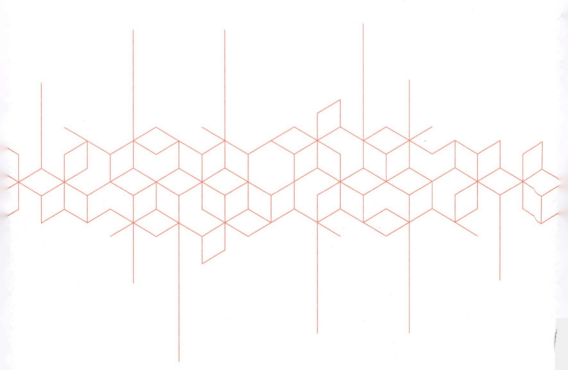

For Mauro, Rachel
and all others who are making a difference

GAME CHANGER

HOW EDUCATION, TECHNOLOGY AND CLIMATE ACTION CHANGE THE WORLD

Koen Timmers

Millions of students and teachers push for a better climate

COLOPHON

Cover design and book design: www.artitude.be

© 2023 Publisher ASP nv
(Academic and Scientific Publishers nv)
Keizerslaan 34
B-1000 Brussels
Tel. + 32 (0)2 289 26 56
E-mail: info@aspeditions.be
www.aspeditions.be

ISBN 978 94 6117 540 3
NUR 130
Legal deposit D/2023/11.161/118

No part of this publication may be reproduced and/or published by means of print, photocopy, microfilm, on electronic or any other manner also without the prior, written consent of the publisher.

CONTENT

Preface - Dr Jane Goodall OBE	9
Recommendations	14
Introduction	20
A word of thanks	21
1 The refugees in Kakuma	23
2 Climate Action Project: getting started	37
3 The fourth industrial revolution: an opportunity	53
Phenomenon 1: everything becomes interconnected	54
Phenomenon 2: privacy	55
Phenomenon 3: the search for other jobs	56
What is the consequence for education?	57
Five crucial skills	58
Creativity	58
Critical thinking	58
Cooperating	59
Empathy	59
Problem-solving thinking	60
Conclusion	60
4 Authentic learning: knowledge and skills	63
Learning is more important than teaching	63
Learning in different ways	65
The importance of pedagogy	67
A. Direct instruction	67
B. Self-discovery learning	69
C. Project-based learning	71
D. Learning by building	71

	E. Social-emotional learning (SEL)	72
	F. Systems thinking	73
	G. Motivation	74
	Conclusion	75
5	**The power of collaboration**	**79**
	Communities of Practice (CoP)	84
	Building walls	85
	CoPs in the Climate Action Project	86
	Conclusion	87
6	**Reinforcing learning through technology**	**91**
	TPACK: successful integration of technology in teaching	92
	SAMR: evaluating the added value of technology	95
	Trend or gadget?	97
	Gamification and game-based learning	98
	Wearables: learning with VR and AR	100
	Artificial intelligence (AI): the chatbot	101
	Why memorise facts when you have Google?	102
	Resistance to technology	104
	Conclusion	104
7	**Behaviour change and mindset**	**109**
	Individual responsibility	109
	Mindset	111
	What drives people?	112
	Maslow	113
	Conclusion	113
8	**The image problem of climate change**	**117**
	Climate	117
	The solution	118
	Communicating climate change	119
	From communicating to teaching	123
9	**The need for climate education**	**127**
	The impact on young people	127

The usefulness of climate education	128
Small actions	129
In figures	129
Momentum	130
Change lifestyle	130
How young people can influence their parents	131
Conclusion	132

10 A big step: Climate Action Project — 137

From idea to action	138
Green Fingers	139
A whole range of activities	140
In the news	142
Cooperation	143
PPP	143
The sky is the limit	144
The power of cultural diversity	145
Conclusion	156

11 Climate Action Day — 149

12 Impact — 159

13 Solving world problems through education — 165

Building blocks	165
1 Knowledge	165
2 Skills	166
3 Student-centred	166
4 Action	167
5 Problem-solving	167
6 Technology	167
7 Culture	167
The PBL roadmap to tackle world problems	168
STEP 1 Make sure you are well prepared	168
STEP 2 Set up projects with a good cause	169
STEP 3 Make projects highly collaborative and socially engaging	169
STEP 4 Keep equality and accessibility at the forefront at all times	170

STEP 5	Share experiences and celebrate impact	170
STEP 6	Make projects transformative	170

14 From teacher to NGO   173

15 Future   179

Afterword - Princess Esmeralda of Belgium   185

References   188

PREFACE

Dr Jane Goodall OBE

I once spoke to a seven-year-old Burundian boy who came to me after I had given a speech at his school. He asked me: 'If I pick up a piece of rubbish every day, then I will make a difference, won't I?' I replied: 'Then you will definitely make a difference.' He smiled delightedly. Then I said: 'Well, imagine convincing ten friends to do the same.' His eyes got very big and he said: 'Wow, that would really make a big difference.' He was excited. Finally, I said: 'Then imagine if those ten friends also convince ten friends each - then a hundred people would pick up litter every day.' His eyes widened even more and were full of wonder. 'What a huge difference we would make,' he said.

We are going through difficult times, socially and physically. There is the climate crisis, there is the loss of biodiversity, and on top of that there are the COVID-19 pandemic and wars. The irony is that we have done all this to ourselves, by having a complete lack of respect for nature. I have spent many years studying creatures that are genetically very closely related to humans: chimpanzees. They behave just like us, in so many ways. But we are different and the biggest difference is the enormous development of our intelligence. Chimpanzees and many other animals are far more intelligent than science ever admitted, but they can never compete with someone who created, say, the internet. We are the most intelligent creatures on earth, yet we have lost wisdom. We no longer make decisions focused on future generations or the health of the planet. We destroy forests and pollute oceans - which are nevertheless the lungs of the world, producing oxygen and absorbing carbon, regulating rainfall and temperature.

Recklessly, we burn fossil fuels and pump large amounts of CO_2 into the atmosphere, causing greenhouse gases to trap heat from the sun like a blanket around the world. We pollute air, water and land. We destroy more and more through industrial agriculture with monocultures, genetically modified organisms and toxic chemicals sprayed on our food. We are putting billions of animals in cattle factories that all need to be fed, need water and who produce a lot of greenhouse gases. We are destroying more and more of our nature by building dams and cutting down trees, by mining and by letting cities keep expanding, with fertile soil under thick layers of concrete.

I once saw a huge ice floe melting in Greenland, icebergs breaking off and falling into the ocean, and talked to people who had to leave their homes because of rising sea levels. I saw the effects of tornadoes getting worse and worse, and the effects of floods and droughts. And the impact of forest fires that killed millions of animals and destroyed homes.

It is absurd to think that we can allow unlimited economic development on the planet with limited natural resources, or that GDP (gross domestic product) is more important than protecting nature for future generations. In some places, these resources are already being consumed faster than nature can restore them.

We clearly need a new relationship with nature. We need to understand that we are part of it and that we depend on it for clean air, water, food - everything. We depend on these healthy ecosystems, which in turn depend on the complex relationships between plants and animals that make up biodiversity. When too many species go extinct, the ecosystem can collapse. Today, we are in the sixth wave of extinction caused by human activities.

The COVID-19 pandemic was the result of the lack of respect for nature and animals. We create situations that allow viruses to pass from animals to humans. The perfect conditions for this are created in places where exotic animals are traded for food, medicine or as pets, and in unhygienic conditions.

We clearly need a greener economy. We need a new mindset. One that puts sustainability first, and sooner rather than later. We need to redefine success. Today we call someone successful who amasses a lot of money and power. But it should be someone who lives comfortably but not extravagantly, someone who spends time with family, in nature. The good news is that we still have time to right our wrongs, to slow climate change and biodiversity loss. But that time is dwindling fast. We need to act now and solve some big problems.

We need to reduce poverty, because if you are poor you are almost forced to cut down the last trees so you can make money selling charcoal. We also cannot afford food being very cheap due to unfair wages and child labour.

We need to tackle unsustainable lifestyles and big consumption, waste and materialism. We need to get rid of our selfish society, which creates so much waste and throws away food while others go hungry.

We need to think about our growing population numbers. Today there are 8 billion of us and by 2050 there may be 10 billion. If we do not change anything, there is little hope for future generations.

And we must ensure that all schools teach about the environment and include ethics in the curriculum. An education system where children have fun and learn by doing. Give children a chance to talk about their ideas, to experiment and explore ideas. An education system that also promotes discipline. Children need teachers who can inspire with stories and encourage them individually. Teachers who detect children's potential and help them realise their dreams. Teachers who make them realise that life is about more than academic success. After all, it's about making a positive difference in the world.

Learning outside is very important, especially for the youngest children: making them connect with plants and animals and making them realise how wonderful nature is. And how much can still be discovered. Once they see that, they will start to love their environment and want to protect it. We need to recognise that many wrong decisions are made through ignorance. It is not their fault that they received poor education.

Back in the 1980s, I travelled to many countries to raise awareness about what was going wrong. I kept meeting students who seemed to have lost hope. They were mostly apathetic; some were depressed and others angry. They told me that we had compromised their future. And that's right. A famous statement by David Brower goes that we did not inherit our earth from our ancestors, we borrow it from our children. But when you borrow, you intend to pay back. We, on the other hand, have simply stolen it. We are stealing the future of our youth. The students lost hope because they felt helpless. After all, there was nothing more they could do to change things. That is why I had the idea of founding Roots & Shoots: a humanitarian programme on sustainability, for young people, by the Jane Goodall Institute. The biggest danger for our planet is that young people lose hope. Because then we stop trying to make a difference. Roots & Shoots was launched as an antidote to helplessness by encouraging young people to participate in projects that have a positive impact on the world around them. The key message is that everyone is important and has a role to play in making a difference. And that the cumulative results of thousands and millions of people result in a big impact. The programme is currently running in 50 countries with hundreds of thousands of active groups. From its inception, it was perceived as a holistic programme where each club or group chooses a project to make the world a better place for people, animals and the environment.

Roots & Shoots: the name is symbolic. Imagine each seed and twig becoming a mighty tree. They look so fragile, but at the same time there is so much energy and life force. Twigs making their way through their roots towards water, the trunk overcoming all kinds of obstacles on its way to the light. Eventually, the trees grow taller than the brick walls and rocks to reach the sun. The walls symbolise all the problems humans have caused on earth, as a result of greed, cruelty, lack of understanding and lack of respect.

Roots & Shoots offers a message of hope: young people - the roots and shoots of our society - can break through and solve problems together, making our world liveable. Roots & Shoots is driven primarily by young people. They study local problems and decide how to tackle them.

All the young people today solving problems caused by previous generations are my greatest cause for hope. There are also the human intellect and science, which enable innovative technologies that allow us to live in better harmony with nature and each other. There are new ways of providing education to youth and more people thinking about ways to reduce their carbon footprint. Some are making ethical decisions about what they buy and about making a switch to vegetarian eating. Many people are planting trees and protecting forests. Others are cleaning up the ocean by fighting plastics and other polluting items. More and more people are trying to bring nature to cities so that city dwellers can admire fauna and flora, which improves their mental and physical health.

Fortunately, nature is very resilient. Even places that were completely destroyed will, in time and possibly with some help, support life again over time. More and more countries and organisations are admitting that it is time for change and some are taking a leadership role in this. And then there are individuals whose stories are

Jane Goodall with Koen and son Mauro in 2022

very inspiring. People who try to tackle the impossible and succeed. These are the stories that give our youth hope and make them realise that there are opportunities.

Yet there are still people who feel helpless when they think about all these problems. When they are really depressed and wonder 'what can I do as a single person?', I refer to that young Burundian boy: take action, go to your community and do something you are interested in. Realise that you and all your friends can make a difference. By rolling up your sleeves, you gain energy. And you inspire others to do the same. And by doing so you begin to realise that we can change things.

We cannot do this alone. We need everyone who cares about our future generations to work towards a new, green economy that is has a less destructive impact on our environment. Then we can solve world problems together. 'We can and we must.'

RECOMMENDATIONS

James Alix Michel, former president Republic of Seychelles

There can never be enough emphasis on education. Education is the salvation of our planet against the dangers of climate change. It is key in the global fight against climate change, which is becoming increasingly urgent. Knowledge about this phenomenon helps young people understand and address the consequences of global warming, encourages them to change their behaviour and helps them adapt to what is already a global emergency. It creates awareness of the existential problem and the need for governments, stakeholders, communities - in short, all of us to take action to stop this existential threat. Empowering the young generation will ensure the future of humanity.

Matt Larsen-Daw, WWF United Kingdom

Young people in education today face a frightening environmental crisis they did not cause themselves. But their future will not only be defined by climate impact and adversity, but also by transformation. As society is forced to respond to climate change by rapidly moving to a green economy, there will be opportunities for those young people who have the skills, knowledge and determination to lead, innovate and shape this future. If schools rise to this challenge, they can ensure that young people enter the world with love and respect for nature. That they have an understanding of sustainability and social justice and an understanding of the skills and knowledge needed to thrive with nature, rather than at its expense.

Andreas Schleicher, OECD

Although students show a high level of awareness and interest in the future of the planet and take responsibility for it in their daily lives, they do not feel a sense of empowerment and choice to really make a difference. Schools need to do a better job of helping students develop a sense of choice and responsibility. I know some will say that the climate challenge is far too urgent to pin all our hopes on the next generation. And yes, that is true. But the slow progress we see with changes in public awareness and behaviour shows how much harder it is to unlearn comfortable beliefs and habits than to get it right from the start. That is why it is important to be green at 15.

Dr Richard Pountney, Sheffield Hallam University

The role schools should play in climate education is often contested by curriculum stakeholders, who disagree not only about learning about climate, but also about the individual and collective response that might be possible. Curricular activities such as the Climate Action Project are an important approach to teaching climate change in schools to instil environmental awareness. And they also provide resources and initiatives for schools to get involved. It is also crucial that schools and curriculum respond to immediate and local needs, rather than seeing climate change as a future problem, something far away. What we need are citizens informed by an educational action plan, led by teachers, to nurture democratic and caring classroom communities.

Dr Jennifer Williams, co-founder TAG

We are in a moment of global intersectionality. Our past and our future, our planet and our individual lives, our behaviour locally and globally - they are all part of an ecosystem. An ecosystem where there are not individuals living in one particular place, but global citizens with the potential to contribute as active parts of society. Today's youth seem to understand this better than anyone else. They recognise that it is no longer enough to avoid negative behaviour, but that it is also essential to take positive actions for the health of our planet and our humanity. As part of this, young people today are demonstrating the power of ingenuity, compassion, innovation and unashamed determination in their work for progress. They go a step further and demand that we all understand the importance of taking good care of our environment and spreading knowledge through quality education. For many educators, this is exactly the moment we have been striving and hoping for.

Christina Kwauk, researcher

Climate change is a contemporary problem with a lack of collective action. Yet students and teachers worldwide have taken action, from the steps of town halls to digital platforms, showing that such action is possible. This book gives us a glimpse of the place where we should focus our hopes for humanity on: the classroom. It shows that the building blocks of collective action begin with an education that is more than just knowledge transfer, but is about making connections between people and communities, about solving local problems with local solutions, and about linking planetary health to social well-being. This book channels the collective energy of students and teachers and is what we need to make meaningful change today and tomorrow.

Marc Goodchild, Cartoon Network, Climate Champions

Working in children's television and digital media for the past 20 years has taught me never to underestimate children's determination to improve our planet - both from a social and environmental perspective.
Today's Gen A and Z live without cynicism, a phenomenon that often derails adults. But they also know their limits and often turn to older teen or adult role models who can help them find their voice.
Media can obviously play a big role, solving the problems, helping to educate and inform, while also delivering facts in authentic, entertaining formats that children already love. We created Climate Champions to mobilise Cartoon Network fans and get them to take small actions. We often hear that children are experiencing more and more 'climate anxiety' because they feel they are 'too small to make a difference'. Addressing this on the ground is essential. As part of our research, we have met some amazing teachers who are already actively making a difference. But it is still very variable, depending on school set-ups and education systems.
So let this be a call to all brilliant educators, to take the bull by the horns and empower the young evangelists of tomorrow, show them the science and help them find their voice, so that they can hopefully drive the urgent social changes the planet so desperately needs.

David Pallash, Build the Change, LEGO

At the LEGO Group, we want to inspire and develop the builders of tomorrow. This has been our mission for many years, but it has never been more relevant than now. The future is uncertain, full of challenges, some of which we have predicted and some of which are just out of sight. Children - with their innate creativity, their boundless imagination, their ability to see a problem as an opportunity to innovate, to test, to fail, to succeed - are ready to help. Not all their solutions will be realistic in the eyes of an adult, but they contain the sparks of inspiration that scientists, policymakers and architects, among others, need when designing solutions in the fight against climate change.

We see 'learning through play' as a powerful tool to teach children the skills they need - problem solving, critical thinking, collaboration, innovation - in order to become engaged and empowered global citizens. But we are also aware that children are not always given the opportunity to learn and explore these pressing topics. Children need to feel heard and involved. We all need to integrate their concerns, thoughts and aspirations into decision-making processes traditionally reserved for adults. We need to prove that we value their ideas and must lead by example. It is their future and they must be involved in shaping it.

Richard Davis, NASA

We can fully solve the biggest challenges of our time, be it global warming or exploring our second planet, Mars. But we need the energy and creative ideas of students around the world. Innovative programmes like Koen's are crucial to growing so many brilliant young children in Africa and contributing significantly to these efforts. I would not be surprised if one day a student of Koen's walked on Mars.

Roman Krznaric, philosopher and author

Education or climate change: which is more important? In this inspiring book, Koen Timmers - one of the world's leading ecological educators - reveals what it takes to create grassroots movements for change, powered by the energy and innovation of young people. A book for every teacher, every student and every concerned human being on this planet.

Thomas Anthony Jones, actor Grey's Anatomy and other productions

My passion for climate change was sparked by Koen Timmers. I thought I was aware of the environmental challenges facing our world until I met Koen at Climate Action Day. Since then, he has armed me with scientific facts, and continues to do so, in an age of doubt and misinformation. Role models may encourage us to live our best lives, but Koen actually inspired me to live for others. He made me willing to throw myself unabashedly into the climate issue. His zeal showed me that climate change is not just about me or my neighbourhood. It is about everything, everywhere and everyone, including people who do not share my views. In short, he made me care. Imagine if we all did.

Marijke Schroos, GM Microsoft Belgium

Education has a vital societal role to play: teaching how to learn, fostering critical thinking, promoting collaboration, embracing failure, and mastering the proper use of technology. These attitudes are not only essential for creating a better world but also for addressing pressing issues like climate change. I passionately urge for the full empowerment of both educators and students, believing firmly that it will yield a revolutionary impact. I envision a world where enthusiastic, well-informed, and fully empowered young minds guide us towards a brighter, eco-conscious tomorrow.

Baron Olivier Vanden Eynde, Founder of Close The Gap

The author brilliantly emphasises the importance of youth engagement in addressing climate change. Through captivating storytelling, the book showcases the transformative power of climate education, highlighting how it equips young adolescents in the Global South with the tools to overcome challenges.

RECOMMENDATIONS

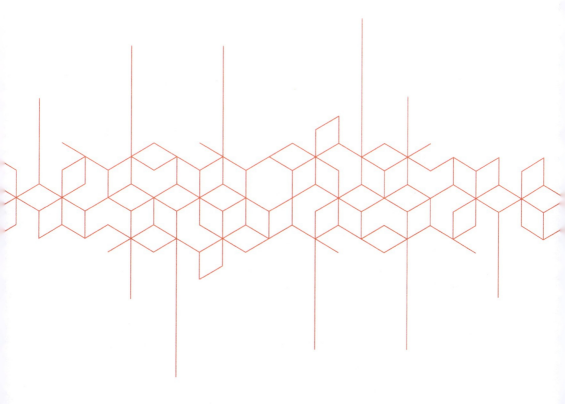

INTRODUCTION

I have had the privilege of meeting many *game changers* worldwide over the past few years. Greats of the world, authorities in their fields, superstars, world leaders. Their voices and their support were a megaphone and a spotlight on my humble efforts to connect education, technology and climate action. But perhaps even more important were the conversations and meetings with hundreds of students, teachers and educational supporters with a big heart for education and this planet. The real stars in my story.

Partly due to the technological developments of the past decades, the world became a village. Through Skype, Zoom, Teams and other digital platforms, we can connect with people thousands of kilometres away from us, whatever their cultural background, their economic situation, their (geo)political context. A laptop and an internet connection suffice, although neither the former nor the latter can always be taken for granted, as you will read later in this book. Partly thanks to these technological advances, education can flourish, regardless of all barriers, even and especially in the 'least-developed countries'.

Education is the engine of growth and progress, collectively and personally. It allows people to gain and share knowledge and skills, propelling an entire community forward. From Malawi to Colombia, from Hasselt to Kakuma. Education informs, inspires and stimulates, offers an expanded view of the world, stimulates creativity and (self-)awareness.

Awareness, for example, that our planet is groaning under climate change. And that urgent (climate) action is needed, to protect the generations yet to come from climatic and all ensuing calamities such as social inequality, climate flight, poverty. Climate action, grounded in creative solutions that, thanks to education and innovation, can kickstart not only politicians but all of us into consciousness for the benefit of the most vulnerable among us.

In this book, I describe how, as a teacher - somewhat naively - I tried to make a small difference by building a school in a refugee camp. And how this eventually led, via other initiatives, to a real movement of millions of people making a positive difference through education in every continent. I explain how I managed to mould this concept into a model that can be used and reused in other contexts to tackle the negative effects of climate change and other social problems.

I dedicate this book to all *game changers* around the world, wherever they are and whatever language they speak.

> Questo è l'ombelico del mondo
> E' qui che nasce l'energia
> Centro nevralgico del nuovo mondo
> Da qui che parte ogni nuova via
> Dalle province del grande impero,
> Sento una voce che si sta alzando
>
> This is the centre of the world
> This is where energy is born
> Nerve centre of the new world
> This is where each new path begins
> From the provinces of the great empire,
> I hear a voice rising
>
> From: L'Ombelico del mondo | Jovanotti

A WORD OF THANKS

You get to know yourself better by raising your child. My son and Rachel give me enormous energy to keep doing this. Even if they have to sacrifice things for it.

1 THE REFUGEES IN KAKUMA

On a hot day in February, I finally arrive in Kakuma. There is always extreme weather at Kakuma Refugee Camp, as it is located in the Kenyan desert. For the past five years, I have been teaching refugees in this camp via Skype and today I finally see them for the first time. During the next week, we will build our own school in the camp that will allow us to reach even more students.

Five years earlier, I was invited to an educational conference held at Microsoft's headquarters near Seattle. Conferences on technology in education usually last three days. There are several speakers and the fact that attendees are well taken care of is an understatement. It usually takes weeks for me to shed the excess pounds. We get sessions on the latest technologies, listen to Malala's father and the CEO of Microsoft. One session is atypical and has an odd title: 'Kakuma'. During this session, we have a Skype call with Moses, a consultant at Kakuma Refugee Camp. The conversation is fraught with technical problems. Against all odds, there are problems in Microsoft's mothership, and not in the refugee camp, where internet connectivity is usually particularly weak. When we are finally able to speak to Moses, he talks about the challenges in the camp and calls for us to help him raise the level of education by teaching maths, English and science via Skype. His plea is touching and I promise to help him.

Once home, I start my research work. I discover that the refugee camp is in north-western Kenya, that it was established in 1992 and has a population of 196 000 refugees (UNHCR, 2021). Many were born in the camp, but new people arrive daily, fleeing war and famine in Sudan, Congo, Somalia and other neighbouring countries. 55% of the refugees are children. Today, there are 13 kindergartens, 21 primary schools and 5 secondary schools, and while 92% of children still attend primary school, only 6% attend secondary school (UNHCR, 2020). Somewhere, things are going thoroughly wrong. The camp is safe and education there is organised by NGOs such as Lutheran World Federation (LWF).

But there is a bigger problem: there are no computers at all in the camp and there is also no internet connection or even electricity. Communication with Moses is also very difficult. Usually, it takes two weeks before I receive a reply to my e-mail. Moses is allowed to use his NGO's laptop and internet connection and goes to another school three times a week. I teach biology classes because they are still somewhat related to my education. Fifteen years earlier I studied this subject, but I have never taught it since. So I usually need five hours to prepare a single lesson, but when I think back to Moses' emotional call, I am willing to do this. It usually takes an hour for us to actually make a connection, and after half an hour, it gets lost in the middle of my lesson. But it was worth every minute. The young refugees soak up knowledge. I discover that they are all very keen on football and we always do a short football quiz, which I also put a lot of time into. Let me just say that it is not my sport. I also use a trick to speed up the communication: I mention that Moses is doing a fantastic job and say that I want to inform his supervisor. From the moment I have his e-mail address, I can send e-mails to two people. I now get daily replies to my e-mails.

The very first Skype lesson to refugees in Kakuma, in 2015

One teacher wanting to provide free, quality education to thousands of refugees doesn't make sense. I put out a call on social media and after six months I can proudly say that we already have a small community of 100 teachers, spread across 45 countries. Some are teaching with their own students, some are not. For teachers in the US and New Zealand, there is an extra challenge: they have to get up in the middle of the night, which creates amusing anecdotes of teachers quickly putting on a jumper and teaching a maths lesson in their dining room in pyjama trousers. These are anecdotes that make the project grow. Screenshots go around on social media, but it takes a huge amount of time before I have a picture taken in a classroom in Kakuma.

Meanwhile, I learnt a lot more about the camp. Classrooms often have two hundred children. Only one in 10 students has a textbook. Even pens are coveted commodities. The upside, though, is that the official Kenyan curriculum is used, the language of instruction is English and tests are standardised as well. Only 33% of teachers are trained and certified. As many as 80% of the teachers are refugees. They are paid a salary of $80 a month. Education is crucial. Every year, several thousands get the chance to start a new life. Those who are the most educated are at the front of the queue. But skills and knowledge are also required to survive in the camp. People in the camp don't give up. They set up small businesses and try to get ahead.

Then disaster strikes: Moses' NGO decides to call it a day. The project becomes bigger than they initially dared to expect and they literally pull the plug. I only just manage to get an e-mail address from one of the teachers: Abdul. I have to make an important choice: leave it as it is or start all over again. At such key moments, I can only recommend not giving up. Try to set your mindset so that succeeding is the only option. I decide to send my own laptop to the camp and learn another important lesson: passing a laptop through customs costs me three times the purchase price of the device. We use a 4G modem for internet connection and electricity is generated by diesel generators. I believe that in the future we should be able to approach this in a more sustainable way.

The project was given a name and a website: 'Project Kakuma'. Our community grew to 525 teachers from 75 countries. My role shifted more towards coordination. Some teachers wanted to do more than teaching only. They wanted to help solve problems like connectivity and streamline processes. Teachers needed to be informed and we had to avoid it becoming just 'waving sessions': young people worldwide speaking to refugees for once, without the refugees learning anything. Teachers were hugely inventive. An Indian teacher sends STEM kits that can be used to make small robots. A Spanish teacher even teaches physical education and during other lessons, songs are written and sung. Sometimes there are tougher moments. Finnish teacher Paula Vorne is asked how many times she eats a day. The refugees say there is one meal a day for them. We also have to make sure they don't become an oddity 'global students' take pictures of with fancy smartphones. The lessons go beyond knowledge transfer. They become intercultural exchanges. I too gain new insights and the project becomes a voyage of discovery. But the internet remains a weak point and there is no immediate solution. There are cheap 4G bundles that are inadequate and there is the high-speed internet via satellite that costs $3,200 a month, an insane amount. Only the UN has this expensive internet connection. Fundraising is difficult. Few organisations appear to be interested in what we do. We depend on funding from our own pockets and an extraordinary donation from people who are involved: crowdfunding, in other words.

Argentinian teacher Jennifer Verschool involves 400 students in her classes and finds that young people's ownership improves when they can do fun activities that have a real impact on the world (Verschoor, 2020). She is invited by the Massachusetts Institute of Technology (MIT) to present the project. A Canadian teacher is also presenting the project in a conference. Our teachers are now starting to get opportunities by being involved in this world project.

When teacher Abdul receives the laptop, he is the king of the world. I can now contact him through WhatsApp and he introduces me to Mohammed Hure, who is an education coordinator at UNHCR. I should have had this connection much earlier, because like every country has a government, every refugee camp is managed by the United Nations Refugee Agency (UNHCR). I can communicate on two levels: directly with the teacher and directly with Hure, who at a higher level ensures that schools are involved in a structured way. Abdul was born in the camp and his family once left Somalia. He is very driven and after only a few months he has good news: he gets to go to Georgia in the US with his family. He will become a cameraman there. Once again, we have to look for a new teacher. And again fate strikes: the laptop disappears. For the second time, we have to start from scratch.

At that point, I am approached by Belgian architects from the firm DMOA, who propose building a school in the camp. Our collaboration pays off: they are very adept at fundraising and building shelters suitable for refugee camps. After all, no permanent structures are allowed to be built there. Then my connections with the UN and the fact that the project is now frequently in the media offer other opportunities. It has always been my wish to do more in the camp than virtual interactions only. I would also like to train teachers and work out a separate track with programming for young adults. In addition, I had the idea of opening the school after school hours as a learning centre where young people could access information on laptops. In our community, apart from live virtual interactions, many teachers turned out to be interested in recording instructional videos. The advantage of this is that they can be re-watched thousands of times at a time that suits teacher and student. A separate group of teachers have started to develop video materials explaining subjects of maths, English and science from the Kenyan curriculum.

We see it big: we will build two schools with solar panels. The schools will be 100% modular and climate neutral. I count on a hundred laptops. We also find an excellent way to cooperate with the UN: they use our solar panels and we use their high-speed internet connection. Still, I want a backup for this internet connection. Suppose we have no connectivity, there would be no project and therefore no education. An empty building, no one wants that. I am discovering that a huge amount of technology is being developed for 'the last mile'. These are usually remote places where there is no internet and technology.

I buy a Rachel device that can hold a huge amount of data and make it available to 50 laptops in one room. A local internet, you could say. The name could not be more appropriate, my smart wife is also called Rachel. Wikipedia, TED, the Khan Academy and many textbooks are already on it. The clever thing is that I can add new resources to it from the comfort of my home, whenever some internet is available. When there is no internet, teachers and students still have access to a lot of information.

In New Zealand, the joke exists that sometimes they can't even be found on a world map. I decide to draw a map where the country is in the centre. It also catches the eye of Helen Clark on Twitter. Clark endorses the project. She is a former prime minister of New Zealand and head of the United Nations Development Programme (UNDP). Princess Esmeralda of Belgium is also backing the project. This support makes it more attractive for newspapers and television stations to report on projects. Add a nice anecdote and figures and make sure the story is local too. It is

Our school, six months after completion

During the first days at the camp, I teach students how to make a paper kite

thanks to one of these articles that DMOA's architects noticed the project and we can now build our own school.

We land on a dusty runway at Kakuma Refugee Camp with a UN plane. I am delighted to be able to shake Hure's hand. An eight-member Hollywood crew pins a microphone on me shortly. They are going to make a Netflix documentary called 'Heroes for the Planet'. I get a driver for a whole week, and they take me to the UN compound. This is a walled-off site where visitors stay. I am only allowed to be in the camp from eight to six. After that, I have to go to my residence. This is unfortunate because it gives me a chance to help build the school, but not to visit some people in the camp. I unpack my luggage under the eye of a camera. I think back to the trip I took fifteen years earlier. Back then, I won a trip to South Africa with educational software I created at school. It was a trip that would fiercely define my life later. For the first time I took a plane and for the first time I travelled to another continent. I visited affluent and poor schools there. I went on safari and walked past townships, small villages with corrugated iron houses and no fewer than 300.000 inhabitants. An hour later, I was sitting in the pool of a very expensive hotel. My first hotel visit, by the way. I will never forget how quickly the fellow travellers were able to shake off this abject poverty. That moment was the reason why I decided twice to continue with the Kakuma project. After all, the project is not about me, not about the community, but about the young refugees. The students. Who would have thought that exactly twenty years later I would be building my own school? Tracy, the director, asks for an initial reaction. I tell her that the poverty I saw during the drive from the airstrip to the UN compound is even worse than I had dared to imagine. The corrugated iron houses, the penetrating smell, the children wearing torn T-shirts. Tracy says I had only seen the village, not yet the camp itself. What I had seen was a typical remote Kenyan village. Kenya, a country that offers more opportunities and is more stable than its poorer neighbours Somalia, South Sudan, Ethiopia and by extension Congo and Burundi. Kakuma is stable, safe and one of the largest refugee camps in the world. It is often visited by world leaders and during my stay, the German president arranged for us to spend a full day, albeit limited, touring the camp. The camp also turns out to be very popular with NGOs and universities, which set up initiatives there and then unfortunately lose interest in continuing them after one year. I am determined to do better and act in a more sustainable way.

I visit a school in the camp and notice the big holes in the walls. The students don't even need to enter through the door. I do an activity with the two hundred children: we build a paper kite and test whose design goes the furthest. For many, it is their first time doing this. We go to another school, once sponsored and built at the request of actress Angelina Jolie. Inequality also prevails in the camp. The school accepts only young girls, who are educated at a high level. They have just won a presidential prize for diction. With them, I do an activity with the Foldscope, a cardboard microscope that costs just $1. My lesson is well-prepared. I brought 20 blades of grass and 20 hairs from my son Mauro. He didn't seem to mind that I took a lock of golden hair from him. Teaching these classes gives me enormous energy. I feel honoured to be given this opportunity. People are enthusiastic. Perhaps one of the biggest misconceptions is that refugees are surly and sad. But these people want to move forward. After a fantastic day, it is time to go to the compound. Actually, it is the same experience again: I go from extreme poverty to a place where food and drink are abundantly available. Only the swimming pool is missing.

After a week, we open the school and this includes coverage by Radio Kakuma and the planting of a tree. My two consultants, Franco and Nhial, keep an eye on things and supervise lessons on site. We now have the infrastructure to roll out various programmes:

- virtual interactions between learners in Kakuma and learners worldwide;
- lessons by teachers worldwide;
- video lessons in maths, science and English;
- An ICT club for young people who want to learn how to use a computer;
- Training teachers together with the University of Nairobi.

Only teaching about programming proved a little too optimistic. No youngsters saw a laptop up close before. Hopefully it will not remain a dream.

The Kakuma project gave me various insights. That African refugees often smile more than people who can carelessly meet their living needs, for example. They remain optimistic despite their difficult living conditions.

But also that many teachers worldwide want to do more than just teach their own pupils. Some also want to take the project to the next level by helping to find solutions to precarious problems. My personal experience is also that determination is

A student at Angelina Jolie's school takes a break from the crowds with her cardboard Foldscope microscope

crucial to achieve a good result. And that technology can make a huge difference, that a simple application developed to make phone calls can achieve something completely different in a different context.

But the most important insight was that - although the main intention was to provide free quality education to refugees - we found that they give something back that may be worth even more. They give an authentic look into their lives - firsthand - to young people who often live in other continents. Young people who often face media where refugees are portrayed in a bad light. Our project has no ambition to directly teach the opposite. We do not ask them to memorise definitions of refugees that paint a more nuanced picture. No, we offer 'global learners' an experience. An exchange that provides new insights. And then these learners choose what to do with it. And we noticed from conversations that took place after these virtual interactions with their teacher(s) and parents, that the students' mindsets changed.

I make a sketch to try to fathom what happened here.

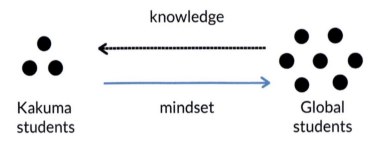

So the initial idea was that we would provide knowledge to refugees worldwide through interactions between students, in order to raise the level of education in Kakuma. The results of standardised tests show that this did happen. Mission accomplished. But there was another unforeseen outcome, which is worth more to me. We changed the mindset of students worldwide. They now view refugees differently and this became our unique way of addressing a growing global danger: polarisation. It is a phenomenon fuelled by intolerance and fake news. It is the easiest way to deal with people you don't understand because you have never spoken to them. Polarisation is a tool for leaders to bind voters to you by first spreading fear. It is something that pops up on social media and is amplified by their current algorithms. It is a danger that causes inequality that is very difficult to undo. Polarisation often has a consequence after which it naturally subsides: conflict.

So I can only applaud the fact that we have been able to both tackle polarisation and provide refugee education through intercultural exchanges. But what if you could also apply this simple model to another problem? To a problem everyone is talking about? Something that young people in particular are passionate about? Climate change. What if the same thing happens here too: that students do more than learn about climate and that there might even be a mindshift with a change in behaviour? The **Climate Action Project** was first launched in 2017. In this book you will learn whether the model works here too and what its impact is.

During my stay, we do a virtual exchange with Irish students

Students who choose to learn to use a laptop can do so in an ICT club

Jane Goodall at the opening of our first Tanzanian school

In January 2020, the World Economic Forum (WEF) mentioned our school in a prestigious report: 'Schools of the Future: Defining New Models of Education for the Fourth Industrial Revolution'. The WEF describes the school in Kakuma as 'one of 15 schools worldwide pioneering the future of education'. Honestly, this recognition is gratifying.

That same year, I decide with Jane Goodall to build two new schools in Tanzania and scale up the initiative. We call them the Innovation Lab Schools. The Tanzanian school is also highlighted in Goodall's documentary on *National Geographic*, 'Jane: The Hope'.

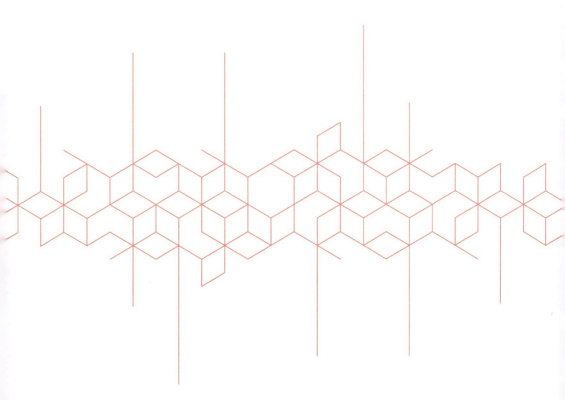

2 CLIMATE ACTION PROJECT: GETTING STARTED

When people talk about youngsters and climate, they quickly think of young people running around the streets screaming and holding colourful signs and bold slogans. For many, Greta Thunberg is the epitome of young people who want to do something about climate change. Admittedly, it may be because of these initiatives that people are now talking about climate change in living rooms. But she herself, in her latest book, questions whether she has ever had an impact on politicians' decisions. I personally have always strongly believed that young people have the potential to do more than raise their voices and kick the shins of the establishment. Young people have the potential to offer solutions and take positive actions for the climate.

Armed with the experience of the Kakuma project, I decided in 2017 to establish the Climate Action Project. It was clear that the project would have to embrace a global dimension from the start. As a primary means of communication, I deployed social media. In doing so, I was curious to see how fiercely people would react to a new initiative. So I decided to send a tweet into the world with a black image and the description 'who is joining a new project?', without any context of what teachers could expect. To my surprise, the message received a hundred enthusiastic responses.

The first edition of the Climate Action Project could count on 250 teachers. The project took place in October because many teachers have the capacity to carry out a project in this month. To some countries this doesn't apply though, as summer in the northern and southern hemispheres does not start at the same time and holidays also fall differently, which in turn affects the start date of the school year. Teachers were instructed to focus on various topics with their students over four weeks: how would you define climate change? What are the causes and consequences of climate change? What would be possible solutions? Particularly this last part was crucial for me. It would indeed soon become clear whether the framework of the Kakuma project would lead to a possible added value here too.

It was not just the Climate Action Project's subject matter that would be different from the Kakuma project's one. The biggest difference lay in the fact that there would be many classes worldwide doing the same project at the same time. There was no direct connection with the students, all communication went through the teacher, who then made the students focus on a particular problem. So a platform was needed. An online space where teachers would not only be informed, but could also post their students' work. In this way, different participating teachers learn from each other's context: are the effects of climate change the same in other countries? What solutions have other teachers worked on? You can find and join this platform via www.climateactionproject.org.

Inclusion was crucial from the start. In order to let people from different continents work together, various actions are needed to avoid clashing time zones, languages, cultural habits and political beliefs. To allow teachers in different time zones to work together, asynchronous exchanges were chosen. By asking teachers to share information via videos, presentations and articles, everyone can learn from each other at a time that falls during school hours. During the final week though we did promote synchronous, virtual interactions. So at this stage cross-cultural exchanges were possible, albeit with some limitations. For teachers in New Zealand, it would be impossible to speak with European or African teachers. And then again, for teachers in the West Coast of the United States, an Asian country would be too big a barrier. In the first year, there was only the capacity to make everything possible in English. Other languages would follow later. A final way to be inclusive is to ensure that people from every continent - including those with very few resources - can participate. That is why we made sure that project participation was free, which was the case from the beginning. In India, Santhi Karamcheti's school participated. In this school, all students have disabilities. In India, people turn their backs on these youngsters. But they too were part of this movement, and the parents were very moved when they heard that their children's findings were being shared and watched internationally. We gave a voice to these youngsters.

A very crucial part of the project is for the students to be at the centre of their learning. This means that they take control and get to decide which direction to take. In doing so, teachers are given a new role. Instead of mainly giving instructions, they should rather facilitate. For most teachers, this is new and therefore a step outside of their comfort zone. And that makes the project less accessible: teaching in a different way and on a more contested subject. Nevertheless, a nice group of teachers

Santhi with her students in India

got to work right away. Most of them were teachers who were already prepared to take that step. They first sounded out students' prior knowledge of the subject and their attitude towards climate change. The aim was not to prepare pupils as well as possible for exams and tests, but to ensure that they learnt a lot in an authentic way. This required them to brainstorm, explore what they already knew and discuss. This allowed them to form an overall vision. It was clear that groups of young people were already concerned about climate, but the climate marches started only a few years after the project was launched. The passion the youngsters had was not to be broken down by the fixed structures of formal education: learning, studying, exams. It was therefore very important to me that the existing passion would only grow by learning about the subject, and that the concern would only be positively influenced by giving young people the feeling that they could effectively do something to solve the problem. In other words, a positive approach. There were no manuals, books, lesson preparations. Just short instructions that were shared weekly. A lot of time was put into coaching the teachers, though. In other words, they were not alone. The lack of a textbook was deliberate. Because a curriculum would immediately push teachers and students in certain directions. It would get in the way of something that was important to me: the fact that students would go beyond learning about climate change to effectively finding solutions.

Students recycling in Vietnam

During the first weeks, it was exciting to experience how teachers engaged with students. I was always looking forward to the short videos they made together, in which they then shared what they had learnt. Often I saw large groups of young people chanting slogans together, with or without flags and other props. Sometimes in dress-up. Then again in the middle of the jungle. And sometimes in sports halls or on playgrounds filled with hundreds of young people and with metres-long banners. A project needs a logo, but so many other things too. The prettier the posters and flyers you share, the more enthusiastic the pupils turn out to be. I remember creating the logo on my computer in just under an hour, not realising that it would subsequently pop up very often in different places. In fact, the Portuguese teacher proudly sent pictures of a mural of the logo against the exterior wall of the school, so that the project would be immortalised. In the photo, she was interviewed by Portuguese national television. Indian teacher Bhavna showed how she made a stamp of the logo with her students. In Peru, Monica sent a photo of a march they held with four hundred students through the city centre. Together they held a banner with the logo, which was several metres wide. Without realising it, they were the forerunners of many other climate activists with their march. In Germany, Marie-Christine did a flashmob with a well-known singer who composed a song especially for the event. And so the logo adorned many places worldwide and masses of people came together thanks to this project.

But the best was yet to come. Another hobby horse for me was that students could develop important skills during the project. After all, the topic allows for creativity, collaboration, critical thinking and problem solving. All these skills could be naturally addressed in the project. Because the project is so open-ended, some teachers even went on to make certain skills the main topic. For example, a teacher in Arizona discovered that her sixteen-year-old students believed everything they read on the internet about climate change. For instance, they found a website where a NASA scientist would claim that the ice in the Arctic was increasing every year. This was a real eye-opener for her, because the news was of course fake. Thanks to the project, she had realised that her students do not acquire information critically at all and believe everything they read on websites. She then dedicated the whole project to critical thinking.

Education is tailor-made. Each age and subject need a different approach. But the project did not offer different guidelines per age and subject. It were the teachers themselves who made it fit into their own subject and curriculum. By 'massaging' the project, they made it relevant to maths, language, science, even physical, and art and design education classes. This required a serious effort from the teachers of course. But we went one step further: by having these experiences shared, we got a very good view of the landscape and new teachers could replicate these efforts. This made it a lot easier for teachers who joined later to participate. Again, this shows that cooperation is important. An organiser must never think he has all the wisdom, but must encourage participation and new influences from the start, while continuing to provide sufficient structure.

For some teachers, the project was a bitter pill to swallow. Climate change remains a topic that arouses strong, often negative emotions for some citizens. Parents and principals who do not believe in it certainly do not want their children to be 'indoctrinated'. In 2017, we saw a special pattern in the United States. We saw a blue circle: all states outside the circle were open to climate education. In the middle states, there were practically no participants. And that had entirely to do with politics. But it went beyond simply having a preference. US teacher Valery even received threats from parents for participating in the project. Her management had even strongly urged her to quit. Years later, with President Biden, we saw a reverse movement. States became more and more open to climate education, and New Jersey was the first state to issue a mandate.

Teachers have been the only source of knowledge in the classroom for centuries. In the process, pupils mainly consumed this knowledge. During the project, we also wanted to explore other avenues. We wanted pupils to learn from each other, but also from experts. And when those experts had a special background or story, that only gave the project more momentum. Our first expert was Céline Cousteau. She is the granddaughter of the famous captain Jacques-Yves Cousteau. Like her grandfather, Céline is an explorer. She combines this with producing films. Together with Jennifer Languell of Discovery Channel, she was among the first speakers supporting the Climate Action Project. Both gave an inspiring speech to students on a different day. Céline spoke about the Amazon and how indigenous peoples are having a very hard time because of recent changes in their environment. Jennifer in turn spoke about how the famous series 'Project Earth' came about and how she and her crew travelled to Greenland for it.

The moment of truth had arrived. Had this project had the same impact as the Kakuma project? There was at least one notable difference: this time we wanted

Tree planting in Malawi

A project for all students: Swedish primary school pupils

to consciously pursue behavioural change, whereas in Project Kakuma, the shell of raising awareness of polarisation came as a bonus.

During the last weeks of the Climate Action Project, the first results of the solutions pupils had found and developed with their teachers came in. Depending on age, pupils had made a beautiful drawing or worked out a concept for a new device. But some went further …

From India, a teacher sent me a picture of her students standing near some kind of go-cart to which solar panels had been attached. I congratulated her on her achievement and their brilliant idea. She responded that it was not an 'idea' at all and that the cart did in fact drive. In other words, her 16-year-old students had developed their own solar car. In Canada, Kristine Holloway went to work with her students and printed coral reefs with a 3D printer after reading that this is an effective way to combat coral bleaching. But there were other finds to generate energy in alternative ways. Ines Rodrigues from Portugal and Ian Fogarty from Canada developed solar lamps with their students. Ian created 3D-printed lamps, while Ines

Nigerian students brainstorm during 2020 Climate Action Project

used PET bottles for them. The lamps were fitted with a small solar panel and a battery so they could charge during the day and give light at night. Ines' students discovered that depending on how much water was in the bottle, a higher wattage of light was generated. Others then went on to cook with solar energy or made a battery that runs on heat. The applications were truly astounding. Knowing that you can make a lamp work on water or on salt, those are things that really make me happy. The WaterLight was developed in Colombia and works for a whopping 45 days on seawater. After that, you just have to pour two new cups of seawater into the lamp. But if you now go a step further and ask teachers to briefly describe all these ingenious solutions, suddenly there is huge potential: all the solutions can be disseminated and repeated via the platform. The only condition is that the resources required are widely available and not too expensive. You can make a solar lamp for $1 and at the same time you recycle a PET bottle, which is a nice bonus.

And the open approach worked. For instance, not everyone focused on energy. Students danced, painted, made poems and composed real songs. In Turkey, Nigeria and India a climate song was created, in Egypt they took the guitar to class. Research confirms that students become more creative when they can apply their knowledge themselves. Pam Burnard (2020) conducted research in Cambridge and argues that pupils should more often put themselves in the shoes of Da Vinci, who perfectly combined art and science. Children can thus link their own experiences to real-world problems to tackle climate change, Burnard believes.

Other groups focused on recycling and waste. In Dubai, large groups of students went to clean up beaches. In Vietnam, Lieu let her students use plastic pots for plants. In Indonesia, Fita let her students make *ecobricks*. This is a way to recycle plastic and turn it into 'bricks'. She collaborated with a big company in her country, making national news.

The results kept piling up. Young people also entered into dialogue with governments. Students in Sweden and Greece managed to get an appointment with the prime minister, where they asked for change during a visit. Ireland's Kate provided perhaps the biggest breakthrough here. She invited the climate minister to her school, where her 11-year-old pupils cited the lack of a clear icon for recycling in Ireland. The pupils got to work and formed 'the green movement'. Today, thanks to their collaboration with the minister, there is a new logo that appears on every item to be recycled across Ireland. The pupils also received a letter from President Michael Higgins, who congratulated them on their work.

Over the years, I have become friends with some participating teachers. For example, Andrews Nchessie from Malawi. Together with his students, he decided to save Lake Chilwa, which was drying up at a rapid pace. By planting trees nearby river banks, they could save the lake. Their plan was ambitious: planting 60 million trees. When a company picked up the news, they created an app for him so that he would be able to track the status of each tree. The president praised the project and gave Andrews a badge of honour. Andrews was frequently in the news,

An Indian student with a solar-powered go-cart

working with the education minister. But that was not the end of his contribution. Together with his students, he developed systems that announce forest fires, made hot water showers by recycling plastic bottles and designed wheelchairs. In the wake of Andrews' actions, several tree plantings spontaneously emerged. It gave Australian Alex Harper and me the idea to build the website PlantED, where tree plantings could be registered. In doing so, people could post the number of trees, location, species and a photo, so everyone could see the impact from each other. The great thing about trees is that they convert CO_2 into oxygen. In this way, they actively contribute to removing CO_2 emitted by cars and factories, among other things. Alex felt it was important to also describe on the website how to 'celebrate' a tree planting. On the site, we showed the calculation of the exact CO_2 emissions that could be avoided by these new trees. It became a success. In no more than two weeks, 1 201 644 trees were planted in 78 countries. Today we are already at a multiple of that; you can see the progress on plant-ed.net.

Irish students received a letter from President Higgins

In Nigeria, students made their own biomass power plants. The 14-year-old students then went to the communities and donated the small power plants so that residents no longer had to light fires to prepare food. Through their action, they saw immediate impact on their communities, making conditions easier and more sustainable. But impact was also created on a larger scale. For instance, the project participants made connections with each other and collaborations emerged across national borders. Mike Soskil heard from a teacher in Malawi that they could not plant crops due to drought. Together with his eleven-year-old students, he found a solution: *aquaponics*. This allows crops to be grown with 85% less water. They sent their solution to Malawi. Mike indicated that this had a big impact on his students. Although they live a few hours' flight from New York, most children had never spoken to anyone from another country. Now their solution was going to help people living on another continent.

A direct link could even be made to Project Kakuma. Teacher Brian Copes made clever things with his students: they made cars, prosthetics and other things. I asked them if they could develop a case with a solar panel, battery and lamp that would allow us to charge at least some laptops. We christened this the *solar suitcase*. In the back of my mind, I thought about the schools in Kakuma, which lack electricity and light. With the project running there, laptops needed to be charged whenever they ran out of battery. In addition, children often spend the night at school. They have to buy candles every day to study in the evening. So the solar suitcase could solve two problems. With justified pride, Brian handed over the solar suitcase in

Screenshot of the PlantED map

Dubai. Australian teacher Ken Silburn, a common connection, eventually brought the suitcase to the camp. Ken did experiments with the students and explained how the solar suitcase works. The design later turned out to have some drawbacks: it was too light to operate an entire school and it sometimes stayed on the roof, allowing thieves to run off with it. Anyway, these students had found a solution for fellow human beings again.

Some solutions really work and make a big difference. But the project is accessible to any age group and everyone works according to their own abilities: pre-schoolers will rather draw and tinker, primary school children make prototypes in cardboard, while secondary school students will come up with effective solutions. In Colombia, students made prototypes of new, energy-friendly cars in cardboard. Such prototypes may not actually work, but they do provide new insights.

With all the solutions found by students - following asynchronous as well as virtual interactions - it became increasingly clear that the model had worked here too. At the Kakuma Refugee Camp, it turned out that virtual interactions between young people and refugees could lead to more than absorbing knowledge. Although the main intention was to provide free quality education, it turned out that the refugees potentially gave more in return by offering an authentic insight into their lives. This changed the mindset of students worldwide. The model was now applied to an-

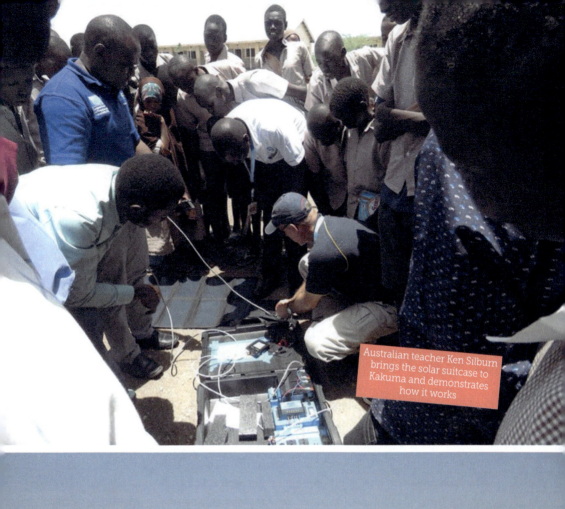

Australian teacher Ken Silburn brings the solar suitcase to Kakuma and demonstrates how it works

Trees are planted in the most challenging places (Saudi Arabia)

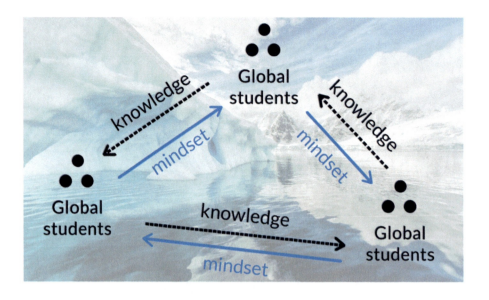

other global problem: climate change. The mindset seemed to change as students came up with solutions. Whether for others or themselves.

In Kakuma, pupils already learnt that fellow pupils in other countries and continents may look different, have a different language and religion. To this day, the differences are insurmountable for some, but they can also be enriching. But especially when you focus on the similarities, you get a connection. And those similarities are always there. They can be habits, or hobbies. There was one certainty: all the students were connected because they focused on the same problem. And climate change also lends itself to that. It is a global problem, with the same cause but with different consequences. But in the case of the Climate Action Project, there was a difference. In Project Kakuma, behavioural change came as a bonus. There was no specific focus on fighting polarisation, whereas behavioural change was at the heart of the Climate Action Project, with young people taking positive actions. The question now is whether this impact is measurable. And how can you measure behavioural change?

In the following chapters, we will find out what kind of education is required to achieve behavioural change. How pedagogy and technology have an impact, and how that impact can be measured. Then we will go back to the project and see what has changed in five years, to finally arrive at a framework that shows how to solve world problems through education.

CLIMATE ACTION PROJECT: GETTING STARTED

Colombian youth doing arts and crafts

3 THE FOURTH INDUSTRIAL REVOLUTION: AN OPPORTUNITY

2017. I chat with my friend Andrews from Malawi. April means that for three years now, we have been invited together to attend the Global Education & Skills Forum (GESF) in Dubai. This is also where the new winner of the Global Teacher Prize is announced every year. We are both lucky enough to be nominated.

We walk past the typical stalls where clever salespeople try to sell their products and services. One stall does have a very large crowd. We see a drone flying in a tube. A while later, it's up to us. I slide a light device over my head and am instructed to concentrate. A few seconds later, the drone flies in the direction to which I direct the device ... with my mind.

Blimey! I was wrongly lulled into thinking that innovation in recent years was limited to televisions and smartphones getting flatter and faster. As it turns out, nothing could be further from the truth. These devices that allow you to control drones, cars and software via thoughts are already available on the market at very affordable prices. This is a typical example of the fourth industrial revolution: new technological developments follow each other in rapid succession.

We are already familiar with the intertwining of global economic, political and cultural processes. We call this globalisation. The fourth industrial revolution is about the merging of the physical, digital and biological worlds. It is the integration of artificial intelligence (AI), robotics, the Internet of Things (IoT), 3D printing, genetic engineering, quantum computing and other technologies (Schwab, 2017).

In the eighteenth and nineteenth centuries, the invention of the steam engine heralded the first industrial revolution. Areas urbanised, production happened on a much larger scale and mass industry was born. The second industrial revolution soon followed. Here, technology with the help of electricity made major advances: cars, photography and light bulbs changed many people's lives. Soon after World

Piloting a drone

War II, there was the third or digital revolution: television, computers and the internet caused a third influential period of change.

Phenomenon 1: everything becomes interconnected

The fourth industrial revolution was announced before it had even started. This honour fell to Klaus Schwab (2017), founder of the World Economic Forum. Research suggests that communication between humans and machines will integrate even further, or even merge. Networks, platforms, devices and people will all be connected. Packages delivered via drones, self-driving (freight) cars, connected communication flows, local 3D printers, AI in warehouses and big data can and will pose a serious threat and challenge to many sectors.

Phenomenon 2: privacy

Another characteristic is that new technologies are succeeding each other at a faster pace and, as a result, leading companies cannot be sure of their position for as long as they were in the past. Remember when everyone thought Nokia was the leading mobile phone brand? Nokia was acquired by Microsoft and died a quiet death. Skype suffered the same fate. Just as every border collie is called a lassie, Skype was a synonym for online calling or 'Voice over Internet Protocol', as it is so nicely called. The same fate may befall Facebook, Google, Apple, Microsoft and Amazon. Possibly in five or ten years, we will be talking about another big five.

An example: the primary purpose of Google and Facebook is advertising, which represents 90% of all revenue. Imagine if other companies found a model from which consumers could also earn. With Google, this is already somewhat the case through their AdSense service. However, what if, when using the service, you are NOT bothered with advertising, but asked if your device while you are online can be used to create a crypto currency such as bitcoin? A new browser that would have remarkable new features while blocking all annoying ads would quickly drive Google's browser off the market. Or what if AI soon gives you an answer to your question, saving you from having to scroll through certain search results yourself?

Privacy is starting to claim its attention again. For now, just because agencies decide it for us. But did you know that Facebook listens to you, Google reads all your e-mails and tracks where you go? Its purpose is to sketch your profile and ensure that the advertising offered matches that profile as much as possible. At this very moment, you are already listed in various databases, possibly as follows: 'lady who drives a cheap car, plays volleyball, works as a web designer and lives in a street with many row houses'. Once we have all had enough of that and an alternative that also offers advantages presents itself, we might switch to other services and organisations.

Phenomenon 3: the search for other jobs

Please google ... Google Duplex for a moment. This new service offers to call the hairdresser on your behalf, make an appointment and put it in your calendar. Without the hairdresser ever knowing she was connecting to a tool.

Which scenario do you prefer, calling a call centre, waiting a long time and running a high risk of not being answered, or calling Google Duplex that helps you instantly? This ever-cheerful virtual voice may owe you the right answer one exceptional time, but the next time he or she will surely know it, after a supersonic search through millions of sources. It is only a countdown to the time when these services will be deployed in call centres.

Several jobs will disappear. Shops will have fewer cashiers due to self-scanning checkouts, you will almost have to take time off work to be helped by a bank clerk, chatbots will help you on online shops and you will check your luggage yourself at airports.

But other jobs will then replace these redundant jobs. Someone still needs to programme and maintain these self-scanning checkouts, chatbots and check-in systems. Here you have to realise two important things: in most cases, this will require even more people. And also, this requires other - sometimes new - jobs with higher profiles. The locksmith who used to make the key to my classroom has now been replaced by a team of people who produce as well as program digital tokens. The craftsman is replaced by savvy whiz kids who juggle with codes. That means people will have to retrain and schools will have to offer different training. McKinsey made the following calculations:

- Only 5% of all jobs will be fully automated, but 60% of all jobs will be slightly changed by automation. Automation and AI will increase productivity and economic growth, and millions of people worldwide will have to adapt and upgrade their skills and occupations.
- 75 to 375 million people will need to learn new skills required by their (new) job.

What is the consequence for education?

That there will be new jobs, requiring different skills, is a certainty. But what are the implications for education? A child born in 2020 might start working in 2040. But do we already know what jobs and technology will be like in these rapidly changing times and consequently what skills they will require? According to Andreas Schleicher (2011), we live in a rapidly changing world where producing the same kind of knowledge and skills will not be enough to meet the challenges of the future. One generation ago, a teacher could still claim that what he or she taught students lasted a lifetime. Today, that is no longer the case. Lifelong learning is becoming crucial. We will have to continuously educate ourselves, and being open to this will help. Several schools are now introducing computational thinking. Young people are learning to think like a computer does, to better understand how to create small programmes on their own. In Hong Kong and the UK, this has been well established for some time. Eleven-year-olds are learning programming there. This skill will become crucial as more jobs will be created that require it. Electric cars, the hydrogen economy, AI applications, biotech and pharma developments require workers with a solid educational base. Both knowledge and skills are crucial here.

But what skills are these? The World Economic Forum (WEF) published a list of skills that will be required by 2030. The top ten include the following skills: analytical thinking and innovation, active learning and learning strategies, ability to solve complex problems, critical thinking and analysis, creativity, originality and taking initiative, leadership and social influence, use of technology, monitoring and control, technology development and programming, resilience and perseverance, reasoning and forming ideas.

In 2019, I got to speak at the European Parliament on innovation in education. An opportunity you don't get every day. Preparations for the presentation took weeks, and it was with nervousness that I launched. Only ... my voice was completely gone. I met Tony Wagner there at the end of the day. Meanwhile, my voice was back and he mentioned that there is a big gap between getting a degree and finding a job. In his book *The Global Achievement Gap: Why Our Kids Don't Have the Skills They Need for College, Careers, and Citizenship - and What We Can Do About It*, he describes that children lack the skills they need shortly after graduation to land a job. In his Survival Skills for Careers, College and Citizenship, he cites seven key skills: critical thinking and problem solving, collaborating across boundaries and leading through influence, agility and adaptability, taking initiative and entrepreneurship, communicating effectively, having access to data and analytical ability, curiosity and imagination.

You can notice a big overlap with skills that also crop up in 21st-century skills: creativity, self-regulation, social and cultural skills, collaboration, critical thinking, problem solving, computational thinking, information literacy, basic ICT skills, media literacy and communication. One might wonder how to decide which skill will be most important in the future. Based on my own experiences in education as a teacher and founder of several global projects, I lift out five, which I would like to explain.

Five crucial skills

The computer will not replace humans, but humans will have to adapt. That requires a set of skills.

Creativity

When I got Lego in the 1980s, you could make anything with these blocks. One day I was making a spaceship, the next a castle. It stimulated my creativity. Today, I buy boxes for my son that only allow you to make the pre-developed design. The Lego pieces are often already no longer blocks and they are shaped in such a way that they allow only one construction. Creativity is more than drawing and playing. It is a skill you need to find solutions, help you out of predicaments and add that fun extra spice to your life. Companies are constantly looking for people who are curious and imaginative. Who think out of the box. A skill that will make all the difference to the machine.

Critical thinking

In the 1960s, the time of the space race between the Soviet Union and the United States, US scientists developed a pen that was supposed to make it possible for astronauts to write even when upside down, in a weightless state and in temperatures as low as 50 degrees below zero.

After $25 million in development costs, they presented this new feat of American technological ingenuity to the world. Full of pride, they asked the Russians what their countermove would be. Their reply: 'We use a pencil.' It is a fantastic anecdote, but sadly enough it is untrue. Such extraordinary stories used to be called urban legends almost affectionately. But unfortunately, fake news has become a scourge of the internet and one of the major drawbacks that innovation brings. Social media allows anyone to have an opinion AND publish it. Not just educated journalists.

Unfortunately, the algorithms of social media like Facebook drive people with similar opinions together, creating so-called echo chambers where fake news can run rampant. But it is not just the written word that can cause confusion. In the film *The Irishman,* actors De Niro and Pacino were given digital make-up and videos of a dancing late Queen Elizabeth II have already surfaced. Deepfake allows seemingly real people to say and do things they have never said or done before. Not only must we learn to detect this and give it a place in our society, we must also learn to deal with it. Language was once a necessary tool for teaching people to cooperate and distinguish social forces within a group. Gossip was the best tool (Harari, 2014). Fake news and gossip are of all centuries. But we must guard against them because they can be a danger to a society. An easy solution in education? Always ask your students to (double-)check their sources. Right from primary school.

Cooperating

There are few jobs in which you do not have to work with others. But teamwork these days is not just about collaborating with the people who happen to be in your office. Technology now also makes it possible to collaborate with people in another classroom, another school, another country or even continent. We devote a separate chapter to it.

Empathy

The ability to put yourself in another person's shoes is crucial. Empathy goes beyond sympathising with someone. It is part of your emotional intelligence. Empathy helps you better understand tense situations, encourage cooperation, better respond to your child's needs ... Empathy enables people to work together (De Waal, 2012).

Marie Miyashiro (2011) also argues that empathy can increase the effectiveness of individuals and teams. It produces better relationships and leads to greater business success.

Problem-solving thinking

In an increasingly complex society, it is important that pupils learn to (re)recognise problems and are able to devise and realise solutions. By focusing on current and future social and global problems, education in all subjects can focus on problem solving as a goal.

Conclusion

When I take the metro in China, I notice that almost everyone is watching videos on their smartphones. A person next to me laughs heavily. He is watching a video of someone eating a crab. Couples leave the metro on autopilot while continuing to watch unperturbed. This kind of rapid consumption of poor information is regulated by social media, which enriches itself with ads. Flashy videos that give a quick high in the cortex and administer a brief dopamine shot there. One might as well offer interesting facts that are equally easily digestible but rich. Information that does contribute to your studies, job and life. The fourth industrial revolution brings opportunities and uncertainty. But gadgets and meaningless information are a first step towards the impoverishment of our society.

People sometimes talk about the Uber, Netflix and Airbnb of education. In doing so, there are two popular assumptions. The first is a plea for the democratisation of education. After all, anyone could teach courtesy of technology. A second plea leads us to believe that there is education 'on demand', where students choose which bits of knowledge they want to enrich themselves with. But you cannot replace a teacher with technology. At most, you can enrich or supplement what he offers. Besides, education is more than mere knowledge acquisition. Especially when teaching about world problems, there are important extras involved, which we will explore in the course of this book.

In our Tanzanian school, we provide students with opportunities to acquire important skills

4 AUTHENTIC LEARNING: KNOWLEDGE AND SKILLS

I have to admit something: I hate homework, but I have recently become part of it myself. Portuguese textbooks teach youngsters about our Innovation Lab School in Tanzania and Kakuma. And that means children may have to memorise my name and write down some key facts in tests. Of course, I understand that evaluation is necessary. Young people need to learn, study and prove that they are making progress. But for some subjects, outcomes other than proving that you have memorised something are desirable. Thus, we want our projects to go beyond knowledge, but also address important skills and attitudes. In this chapter, we explore the pillars of quality education and the importance of learning, knowledge and pedagogy in designing authentic education.

What is actually the importance of education? Is it to succeed on tests, to ensure a nation's economic prosperity, to become happy, to provide your family with an income, to innovate permanently or to solve important problems? Is the objective identical in different countries and would teaching be affected by it?

Learning is more important than teaching.

A lot of experts have already done research on education, but strangely, most research is done on teaching and not learning.

Learning is the acquisition of new or the modification of existing knowledge, behaviour, skills or values and can involve synthesising different types of information.

Someone who has influenced my views on education is Ken Robinson. He gave several haunting but funny TED presentations. Robinson once argued that all children naturally enjoy learning, but that this seems to change with most of them as they get older. Are we doing something wrong in education? We are now studying how people learn and how best to teach.

According to Strong (1995), actively engaged learners are driven by four goals: success, curiosity, originality and relationship. When we dive into research on education, we find that the main focus is on knowledge transfer. And our search through the fourth industrial revolution taught us that skills are crucial. The Kakuma project even led to behavioural change. How can we reconcile all this?

Think back to the time when you were sitting behind the school desks yourself. And recall the teachers. Who do you remember yourself? A teacher determines good teaching. Nothing is more important than an inspiring teacher who knows how to take students to the next level. Nothing is more terrible than a teacher who, over time, loses the passion to keep inspiring students and for whom teaching is nothing more than a job. Good things happen in classrooms everyday thanks to teachers who are aware of their audience, their pupils, and dedicated to teaching efficiently. Different pupils often have different needs too. Improvements in teaching and educational outcomes start with a teacher setting aside time to make change in a classroom in response to ever-changing situations (Brause & Mayher, 1991). After 15 years of teaching, a new world opened up for me after reading Jean Laves' (1996) quote which states that a 'Teacher is neither necessary nor sufficient to produce learning'. With this, Lave affirms that learning is the essence of teaching and not teaching. While this may seem a very simple message, it should be at the heart of policymakers', headmasters' and teachers' decision-making. In fact, Lave's message includes two key components:

- students can learn in different ways, even without teachers;
- education is about students and their learning, not about teachers and teaching.

So how can you learn efficiently, and does this learning depend on content? Unfortunately, when you read through research and opinions, you don't get much wiser. There do seem to be two main camps. One camp argues that the main role of teachers is to convey knowledge clearly. Perhaps this is the way you yourself were educated for years and you may remember it as being rather passive. In the other camp, this kind of teaching only raises a red flashing light; they argue that the teacher has more of a guiding role in a concept where students learn from each other and where a particular problem guides the learning process. Camps are never good. Let us unravel both approaches and find out which way is best now. Or maybe both.

The fact that children just like to eat fries does not mean it is good for them. There is a difference between what we like and what is good for us. A system where the teacher provides knowledge is a model that has withstood centuries. And we are all still alive and have only improved intellectually. But in a few decades, we have made huge strides technologically. Information is now available everywhere. We fly to Mars and are now switching to electric cars. Do all these developments also require changes in education?

Learning in different ways

Did you know that the submarine, the Segway and the parachute already have one thing in common? They were all invented by a person who died from his own invention. Did you know that the typical smell of rain on dry ground is called *petrichor*? And that there is a word for recognising objects in the clouds? Pareidolia. Education can lead to wonder and teachers have the power to tell stories that youngsters will carry with them for decades to come. Peppering lessons with these kinds of fun facts is one way to increase engagement. The older our students get, the less often they seem to be wowed. Is that because of their age or the way we teach? A way that is increasingly academic and where there is less room to discover things for themselves.

There are several ways to make learning happen in students. We focus on two different ways of tackling things. On the one hand, there is direct instruction, where the teacher mainly disseminates knowledge in an efficient way. On the other hand, there is self-discovery learning, where the teacher guides students as they consider a problem they are trying to solve together. A teacher will need to link pedagogical forms of work to this. This could be teaching, demonstration, class discussion, discussion, group work, self-study, or some other form of work. However, there is no golden ratio for this, with the result that in reality different teachers will apply certain teaching materials in completely different ways. Today, teachers (on social media) and researchers (at conferences) are having real debates about what would be the most efficient way. Even at a national level, there are trends, influenced by education ministries.

Australian students learn about climate during music lessons

We also notice this during the Climate Action Project: Canadian and Indian teachers embrace self-discovery learning, while in the UK and Belgium people tend to favour direct instruction.

The importance of pedagogy

Pedagogy is hugely important for a teacher and probably one of the most crucial parts of the curriculum during a teacher's training. This is because there are several options for conveying a subject to pupils: teaching, collaborative learning, field trip, teaching-learning discussion, self-study, corner work, narration, project-based learning … For example, when I have to teach a lesson on traffic, I can teach it in at least three ways: I explain traffic rules at the blackboard, we put on yellow vests and go on an excursion in the city, students are put in groups and each group has to study different traffic signs and present them to the class after some time. Different teaching methods have different advantages and disadvantages. For instance, collaborative learning often takes more time and field trips can come with organisational challenges. Sometimes they are combined and sometimes a teacher makes the wrong decision to rely on a different working form another time. But within pedagogical working forms, there are several categories: offering and collaborative forms, which include direct instruction and self-discovery learning.

A. Direct instruction

Direct instruction is a model of teaching that emphasises carefully planned lessons designed with clearly defined and prescribed learning tasks. The basis of this model lies with the American Siegfried Engelmann. He argues that clear instruction, avoiding misconceptions, will lead to better and faster learning. Pedagogical techniques used in direct instruction include working groups, participatory laboratories, discussion, lectures, workshops, observation, active learning, practicals and internships.

To understand the importance of knowledge, we need to know better how human memory functions. Tim Surma (2019) explains: in terms of memory, the human brain works in two ways: working memory and long-term memory. Working memory is consciousness. This allows you to think. It will remember facts, but has a limited capacity of four to seven places to do so. So when you need to remember 12 letters, working memory is overloaded. Long-term memory is the storage place for all the things you know and can do. This comes to the rescue of working memory when needed. This is because new facts are anchored to knowledge that is already there. Specifically, this means that basic knowledge is crucial because it is constantly being built on. Knowing the multiplication tables, having sufficient vocabulary or knowing the world capitals by heart, it all contributes to learning more easily, more and faster.

Furthermore, prior knowledge should be activated at the start of the lesson and testing should be frequent. And this as much as possible, but assessments with marks are not always necessary, Surma argues. It is essential that the teacher explains this and that students do not discover it themselves.

Pupils in Moldova learn about global warming

B. Self-discovery learning

'Ditch that textbook', 'Learn like a pirate' ... there are a lot of individuals and organisations for whom direct instruction sets off alarm bells. They stress the importance of engagement and the position of learners in their learning process. And they also emphasize that education has the ability to go beyond the information recorded in textbooks.

In self-discovery learning, the teacher clambers off the stage and pupils are guided from the sidelines. 'From sage on the stage to guide on the side' is sometimes called the principle where pupils are placed at the centre of their learning. The method is often project-based, inviting pupils to focus on a particular question or address a particular problem. They often work together, and skills are an important part of the lesson.

Self-discovery, activating or learner-centred learning, these are different terms that belong to the same movement and are roughly synonymous, although they focus on different factors. But they all serve the same purpose: challenging pupils to actively investigate the world; following their natural curiosity. And that is by no means the case for only a handful of subjects. In fact, it is perfectly possible to link lessons in mathematics, history, biology, geography, music and other subjects to such themes. Pupils are given a more active role and are at the centre of their learning process, which they themselves help steer. In doing so, they not only consume knowledge, but also construct it themselves.

While knowledge is very important, education is more than that. First, there are those important skills such as creativity, empathy, problem-solving and critical thinking. In addition, there is motivation. We also need to ensure that students enjoy learning in order to encourage life-long learning.

Self-discovery learning starts with an essential question that allows teachers to address the curriculum while igniting students' curiosity to open a conversation. It emphasises a child's self-efficacy and spontaneity. The programme needs to be sufficiently flexible so that learners' input can lead to further questions and thus start directing the teacher during the learning process (Murdoch, 2010). The latter often takes teachers out of their comfort zone because it can be difficult to prepare and does require some background knowledge on the part of the teacher. It is often a barrier for novice teachers, who are faced with expectations, parents, classroom discipline, tests and all kinds of official documents. In addition, it is still a taboo for teachers to admit that there are things they don't know. After all, all sorts of parties consider you a content expert. But that is what is required when you switch to self-directed learning, as pupils will decide for themselves which directions to take and which subjects to explore in order to do so.

The focus is on students' learning and fuelling their deeper understanding. Learners become researchers accessing information through technology and experiences.

Wolpert-Gawron (2016) points out that generating curiosity when learning something new is crucial, as it leads to enthusiasm. She offers four steps: students develop their own questions that they themselves would like to have answers to, they conduct their own classroom research on those questions, they present what they have learnt and they reflect on the process. I once spoke to a teacher in a Dutch primary school who, on a rolling basis, asked two pupils to make a presentation on

Pupils in Romania seek solution to plastic pollution while tinkering

what they had learnt that day. He indicated that this reflecting worked wonders. The more time passes, the more learning occurs. Doctors refer to specialists faster than before and consequently young people also have to learn more than before. It is therefore impossible to always let them choose for themselves what they want to learn. But within certain times - set by the teacher - this method can certainly be very valuable. Certain elements can also work separately, such as reflection and learning how to make and perform a presentation.

Self-discovery learning will form an important basis for the climate project, where we try to find a good balance between offering knowledge about climate and letting the participants discover concepts and possible solutions.

C. Project-based learning

Project-based learning (PBL) refers to a longer programme where students work on real-life problems to arrive at a tangible solution. It encourages them to design something, solve problems, investigate and think critically. Here, collaboration and communication are crucial, as is a strong work ethic (Pearlman, 2009). Students become active learners, taking ownership for their own learning process as the programme progresses (Savery, 2015). The Climate Action Project draws heavily on this mode of work.

D. Learning by building

During the Climate Action Project, pupils made lots of things. One group of pupils made their own bioplastic, learning to see if this is a worthy alternative to plastic. They also started wondering how plastic items are developed.

In constructionism, you learn by making things. In his book *Mindstorms: Children, Computers and Powerful Ideas,* Seymour Papert (1980) elaborates on Piaget's ideas, in which learning is about constructing knowledge. But, says Papert, there really should be something to go with it. According to him, learning by and with the purpose of making something is the way learning really happens.

Nowadays, this movement, as well as *Maker Education*, is gaining more and more attention and followers. Often, this is also done in project form, involving collaboration. The use of computers allows pupils to create and learn in many different ways.

E. Social-emotional learning (SEL)

Social-emotional learning is the developmental process by which learners acquire fundamental life skills. It involves skills that enable us to shape ourselves, our friendships and our lives effectively and morally (Devaney et al., 2006). They include life skills such as recognising emotions in oneself and others, caring for others and making wise decisions. SEL is important because we need to better understand relationships, emotions and behaviour. We will explore further below how to make this a concrete part of the learning process.

In 2016, I launched the Human Differences project with participating schools in 50 countries. We wondered why countries build walls and whether everyone is equal. I had a bold idea and decided to set up Skype conversations between classes from India and Pakistan, Israel and Palestine, the US and Russia and Northern Ireland and Ireland. Countries that had been in conflict or even war with each other for decades. The conversations always included a moderator from another continent. The students talked about everyday issues such as sports, food, religion and culture. Afterwards, the young people suddenly realised that there are so many more similarities than things that are different. They came to the general conclusion that appreciation for each other had grown greatly. Imagine if we did this on a large scale. Imagine one of these kids becoming the next world leader. Intercultural exchanges have enormous added value, as our Kakuma project already showed, and yet they are not part of the curriculum. Today, they are initiatives that come from teachers who see the opportunities and the added value. It is one way of bringing SEL into the classroom.

What do emotions have to do with learning? Well, a lot, as it turns out. The relationship between emotions and cognition is often underestimated and misunderstood. Emotions and cognition are supported by independent neural processes. The overlap between emotion and cognition is called 'emotional thought' and includes the process of learning, remembering, making decisions and demonstrating creativity (Immordino-Yang and Damasico, 2007). Immordino-Yang argues that it is neurobiologically impossible to remember, process complex ideas and make important decisions without emotions.

AUTHENTIC LEARNING: KNOWLEDGE AND SKILLS

The Skype conversation between Indian and Pakistani students, with New Zealand moderator Jodi

F. Systems thinking

The world we live in is a complex nexus of different systems. Issues such as deforestation, plastic problems, politics and gender inequality are often too difficult to understand at a glance.

Systems thinking is a scientific approach where you try to keep an overview of the whole, rather than focusing on individual parts without considering the role these parts play in the bigger picture. By engaging in systems thinking with your students, you support them in exploring the world. In this way, they develop an understanding of society.

Through systems thinking, the Climate Action Project unravelled the various problems by visualising climate change. Causes and consequences were mapped, along with the different perspectives. Then connections were made with the participants' behaviour, which gave new insights. Thus, many interests and components came to the surface. During the process, it became clear that pupils are also part of the system and can bring about change. This makes systems thinking a crucial skill to prepare young people for today's challenges and those of the future. In the final phase, you zoom out to better understand the overall picture.

When I saw paper bags in shops' produce department replacing the plastic ones, I was delighted. At last, single-use plastics were being acted upon. But the reality is more complex and requires you to start analysing complicated systems. For instance, a paper bag has a much heavier carbon footprint because it requires much more carbon and water. Both the paper bag (trees) and the plastic bag (oil) need raw materials. So if you only look at the carbon footprint, you could argue that the plastic bag is the better choice. But once it ends up in nature, it takes centuries for it to break down completely. In the meantime, the bag is transformed into very small microplastics that often end up in oceans and then our bodies. The correct answer is that a cloth bag is the best option.

Introducing systems thinking in a school is necessary to deal with our increasingly complex society and specifically to teach sustainability. Skills such as cooperation, critical and creative thinking, seeing connections and communicating come into play (Jutten, 2010).

G. Motivation

I took many science classes in my school career, but they could only moderately captivate me. Besides, I certainly do not feel that I am technically gifted and my skills are limited to changing a light bulb. But as we looked for energy-friendly solutions together, I started buying small DIY kits ('do it yourself') with my 11-year-old son to make small robots, but also trolleys driven by solar energy and even salt, a clock that runs on water … Soon we bought a soldering kit and our curiosity was boundless. The essence of the science lessons was the same and I gratefully claimed some core concepts that stuck in my mind, but the approach was quite different.

Nick Fuhrman (2018), in his endearing TED talk 'One thing all great teachers do', tells how he rewards great performances of his 20-year-old students with stamps of eagles and turtles. Although his colleagues at university declare him crazy, he sees how much his students appreciate these stamps. We should also not hesitate to celebrate mistakes. Everyone makes mistakes and therefore they need not always be marked in red. Failure should be allowed, inside and outside the classroom walls.

Conclusion

When I founded the Climate Action Project, I made a mistake. I wanted students not to lose the passion that might have existed for sustainability and climate in the classroom. My assumption was that if they took ownership of their learning, they would gain deeper insights. And they did. But that was not true for every component. The greenhouse effect is a complex concept that needs explanation. In that knowledge transfer, the most efficient way is direct instruction. But in other subjects, pupils should be given the opportunity to be at the centre of their learning, solving problems and exploring on their own. Teachers are then given a new role and must guide their pupils in their quest.

Not everything can be expressed in grades and therefore examined. Yet this is the only way a student can reap success at the end of the school year: with marks. Not everything can be measured quickly and easily. But that does not mean it is not im-

Egyptian students came to school for four weeks during school holidays to still participate in the Climate Action Project

portant for our students. Some components are very difficult to convert into marks, but that does not make them any less important: empathy, creativity, being able to solve problems, cooperation and so on.

Whatever pedagogical working form is used, the teacher has a crucial role. Besides being a content expert, he is an empathetic pedagogical engineer who links the right approach to certain topics. There is no 'one size fits all'. Nor should we be too quick to pigeonhole our pupils. Every age, every subject may require a different approach.

However, when trying to address world problems through education, we must dare to go further and a drastic but sophisticated approach is absolutely necessary. If we want to discuss climate change in the classroom, we need to be informed, discover, learn from each other and possibly even take action. Because climate change requires a behavioural change and mindshift.

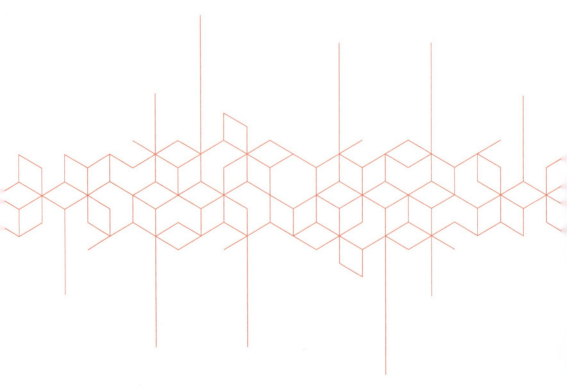

AUTHENTIC LEARNING: KNOWLEDGE AND SKILLS

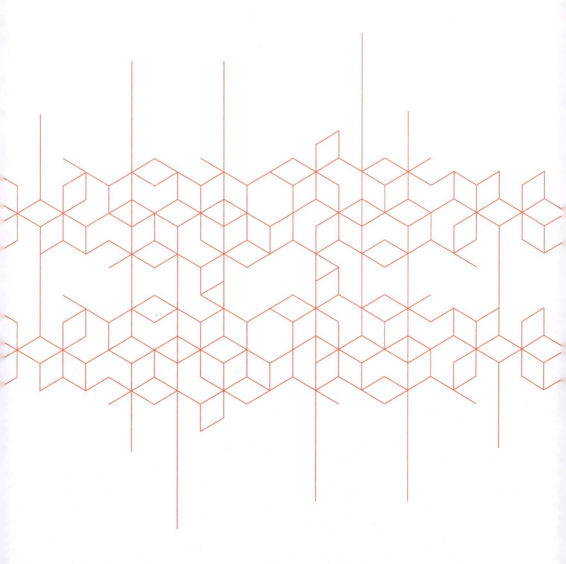

5   THE POWER OF COLLABORATION

Ten years ago, student Andy had the annoying habit of fact-checking facts I was teaching about on Twitter. Sometimes he would dare to tell me that I was wrong and that his Twitter network confirmed it. Although I was a Twitter lover myself, I did not like this negative feedback and my first reaction was to say that the ICT co-ordinator should block social media on the school campus.

I was wrong.

Collaboration is important in every layer of society. For various jobs, it is often unthinkable that a job can be done by one person alone. Yet classroom learning is often an individual activity. Can working together also contribute positively to our students' learning? Brown and Duguid (2000) argue that learning is a social process. Collaborative or social learning is the situation where students learn together, rather than individually, where people depend on each other's resources and skills. In team, people can focus on an important question, explore or create a meaningful project with the aim of learning in an authentic way.

I too learnt about the most common birds through a collaborative work format. Instead of our teacher explaining fifteen birds to us, five groups set to work making their own presentation on lifestyle, food, habitat and external characteristics of three specific birds. There were learning gains. I don't think I will ever forget any detail about the black-headed gull, great spotted woodpecker and barn owl. Whether that applies to everyone in the group, the future will tell. After all, not everyone was equally committed to the task. And to be completely honest, I can't even remember which birds the other groups made a presentation about. But besides that, I did learn how to plan properly, how to give a presentation and how to use PowerPoint myself for the first time. Did I learn much from my group mates? Not directly. None of us had any prior knowledge. We did, however, learn to look up things well together. Research shows that educational experiences that are active, social, contextual, engaging and include learner ownership lead to deeper learning (McGee, 2006).

Kenyan students work in groups during Climate Action Project

Vietnamese students present their findings

There are two main types of collaborative learning. They each have their specificities, advantages and even technologies that can be used in combination with them.

Social constructivism

Vygotsky (1978) suggests that learning is a social activity and that people learn by interacting with each other. Vygotsky and other social constructivists believe that knowledge developed while working together is more than knowledge developed individually. In social constructivism, learners work together to construct knowledge together. Here, it is crucial to learn through authentic problems. Knowledge is not primarily conveyed by teachers, to avoid learners passively absorbing it. The teacher becomes a facilitator and learners are encouraged to interact, exchange views and experiences and together construct knowledge and meaning based on their needs. Learning involves active processes where knowledge is built on top of a foundation of previous learning experiences.

This includes discussing, creating and constructing. Pupils learn in a group. In communities or groups, involvement, trust and commitment of all members are monitored by the teacher.

During the Climate Action Project, students engaged in classroom discussions on climate, focusing mainly on the problems caused. They learnt from each other's insights and prior knowledge, trying to build solutions. Then they presented their findings to the other groups. The teacher guided them and made sure they had the required prior knowledge.

Connectivism

Connectivism is modelled on technology learning by Siemens (2008) and Downes (2008) with socio-cognitive aspects.

Siemens mentions that learning can arise from building networks of information, contacts and resources applied to a real-life problem. Connectivist learning focuses on building and maintaining connections in a network that are current and sufficiently flexible to be applied to existing and emerging problems. In connectivism, there is a central role for relationships and networks. A person builds a 'personal learning network' (PLN), which consists of so-called 'nodes' (similar to a comput-

Filipino youth work together in 'Human Differences' project

er or other device connected to a network). Each resource is called a node from which you can learn: peers, books, experts, a teacher, a website, a blog, etc. The teacher must have the capacity to find and apply knowledge when required. Learners will encourage each other to be involved in the network. Siemens and Downes believe that you can also learn from non-human sources and thus place connectivism in the context of Latour's (1996) actor-network theory (ANT). Learning activities include exploring, connecting, creating and evaluating.

In the Climate Action Project, pupils learnt by looking up information on websites and YouTube, emailing experts and writing reflective blogs. The teacher monitored students remotely and steered them in the right direction if they were on the wrong track.

I remember one class where the teacher worriedly reported to me that collaborative learning was really not working in her group. What went wrong was that the right background was not being outlined. A teacher must always provide the required prior knowledge - often through direct instruction - before proceeding to form groups of learners. Without the required context, collaborative learning does not work.

But not only collaboration between pupils is important. Collaboration between teachers can be equally important.

During an event, I speak to Ivan, a slender person. I could see earlier that he was struggling to strike up conversations with other attendees. He introduces himself as a programmer, and when he learns that I once taught web design classes, another Ivan emerges, enthusiastically throwing terms at me I had no clue about. At the same time, I tell him about my global projects and how technology plays a part in them. How students develop climate education solutions together in virtual worlds and how online students from different continents have the chance to discuss them together. Three years after our conversation, he sends me a message via Telegram. Whether I was the person who told him about that project. He has a message for me: he created his own version of Minecraft for our project, where students can build and experiment in a 3D world.

When people work together, very powerful applications can emerge. Collaboration, teamwork and networking can also be important for teachers. A teacher who can discuss, create and reflect with a colleague in the same school, in another city, country or even continent, can benefit from this in various ways: exchanging teaching materials, gaining new insights, expressing concerns, and so on.

When we talk about a network in an educational context, its purpose is to share knowledge, information and contacts. When I started teaching refugees in Kakuma, I soon became aware of a shortcoming: my limited time versus too many students who had a certain hunger for information. I decided to set up a network. A community of teachers who had one goal: to share knowledge for free with people in need. Soon we had a group of 100 teachers in 45 different countries. All these people were contacted through social networks like Facebook and Twitter. What inspired them to participate? What are pitfalls of communities and how do you achieve optimal results? Are goals achieved in one direction and what are the expectations of all members?

Communities of Practice (CoP)

A Community of Practice is a group of individuals with similar roles and responsibilities who come together to share ideas and best practices (Wenger, 1998). They spend time together discussing important topics, asking questions and sharing answers. It is a support network for individuals with a common interest, set of problems or concerns. They gather to achieve both individual goals and collective goals. The goal is often to develop new knowledge to advance a domain or professional skills. Interaction of longer duration is crucial here. Many communities rely on face-to-face meetings, while also using web-based environments to communicate, connect and carry out activities.

The theory of the CoP was developed by Lave (1991) and Wenger as they searched for opportunities to learn outside formal courses and workplaces. The idea is based on John Dewey's 'Principle of learning through occupation' (Wallace, 2007).

And that is why all the principles of a CoP are put on centre stage. Niesz (2007) argues that a CoP consists of four elements: *community* (learning to belong somewhere), *identity* (learning to become someone), *practice* (learning to do), *meaning* (learning as experience).

In the Kakuma project, we need to distinguish between the group of teachers offering virtual lessons and the community helping with support, coordination and problem-solving. The underlying passion is free education for refugees, the problem is the enormously difficult situation: weak internet connection, hardly trained teachers and difficult living conditions.

The fact that new problems arise all the time and that members are not only teaching but also involved in solving these problems, helping the project grow and sharing these successes with the outside world makes the community particularly engaged. But there is also room to share concerns: a lesson that cannot take place due to poor internet connection in Kakuma, sensitive questions asked ('how many times in a day do you get to eat?') or difficult communication ('there is no class today because of exams'). These make some drop out, but make the majority even more committed to finding solutions to them.

Building walls

In 2016, I launched the Human Differences project. We asked why countries build walls and how we can work better together. The common thread was that we are all equal, but don't always have the same rights. We do need to have equal opportunities. Right from the start, it was clear that there would be tensions. A teacher from Lebanon was not allowed by her school to participate because an Israeli teacher was participating. Lebanon does not recognise Israeli territory. While this shortcoming was precisely the core of the project, it shows that there can be sensitivities about which you cannot judge and you cannot take lightly. There are no nations with bad people. At most, there are bad world leaders. In the Climate Action Project, Chinese teachers were not allowed to participate because the project is supported by the Dalai Lama. In some African countries, students could not participate because they have limited internet connection. And in some US states, teachers who wanted to participate were threatened by parents 'because climate change is a hoax'. For all these reasons, it makes sense never to coerce, but to inform better.

Cultural differences are priceless. And while a cheap plane ticket can get us to another continent relatively quickly, sometimes we know nothing about local customs, religion and culture. The Japanese wonder what the name of a block is, while the American, in turn, must know the name of the street. For both, the other is just the space in between. In China, a doctor is paid when the patient is healthy, otherwise people make the negative connotation between being sick and making money. Cultural differences should be celebrated.

I myself noticed that the cultural factor also contributes to networking. Group members from some countries sometimes have a louder voice. So you have to make sure everyone gets an equal share. You also need to be vigilant that group members do not participate just to get a certain certificate, but that there is intrinsic motivation. Finally, you also have to make sure that commitment remains, even when targets are achieved. In the Kakuma project, we have a group where everyone exchanges experiences, providing rich information for others. Members also help solve problems with connectivity, lesson topics and so on. However, we also come across people who want to teach just one lesson so that a photo can be taken which is then shared on social media ... After that, there is no engagement in the group.

Ukrainian students receive certificate after completion of Climate Action Project

CoPs in the Climate Action Project

Communities of Practice play a very decisive role in the Climate Action Project, but also in the Kakuma project. After a while, I discovered that fifty is a crucial number. When you have to supervise more than 50 schools, you can no longer personally monitor everything and provide the necessary quality. But some teachers wanted to do more than teach their own students and their passion extended beyond their classroom walls. A new concept was born: the facilitator. These people are happy to help translate sources as well as mentor new teachers. A system was developed to select facilitators who had already gone through the project themselves and gained experience in the process. In order to bring teachers together we initially also used WhatsApp, where successes and concerns were shared. Facilitators were really keen to help these people and share their expertise. Others developed activities that others could replicate and help make the project stronger in terms of content.

But some teachers wanted to go even further. They wanted to grow the project themselves by collaborating with partners, sharing their story with the media or by reaching out to the government with the hope that a cooperation could be set up. They were called 'ambassadors'. There could only be one ambassador per country, unlike the facilitators. And ambassadors were selected by me personally. Putting all ambassadors together in a virtual group also allowed them to take each other to the next level by exchanging achievements. This also allowed us to quickly map out the state of climate education in various countries. Or why a certain technology did not seem to be used in some countries. Or what the political sensitivities might be. Ambassadors were given a say in the project and we held brainstorming sessions during online meetings.

Anno 2023, there are 85 ambassadors and 175 facilitators.

Conclusion

During my first world conference in Barcelona, I learnt about it for the first time: the Marshmallow Challenge. A group activity where individuals have to make the highest tower in a small challenge and with just some spaghetti, sticky tape and one marshmallow. The Marshmallow Challenge was created to encourage cooperation between people meeting each other - often for the first time - in a playful but efficient way, and to generate relevant insights. The challenge mainly served as an icebreaker. Three years later, I am speaking in Utrecht in front of thirteen hundred teachers and decide to address different ways of learning using the Lego Duck Challenge. Each participant in the theatre is given a six piece bag of blocks and in thirty seconds they have to make a duck with them. The colour of the blocks and the drawings on them are so specific that it is impossible not to make a duck. It is thirty seconds of pure fun, noise and insight. And afterwards, everyone proudly shows a duck. At least, if the pouch didn't fall under the chair, or the too-short-cut nails managed to open the pouch. I explain that there are as many as 50 million different final results and that there is a huge chance that everyone has built a different duck. The Lego Duck Challenge essentially states that the teacher can do two things: either build their own duck for each student to recreate, or have the participants create and explain their own model so that everyone including the teacher learns from it. In doing so, the large number of variations will be so rich that it will add to the whole.

Now that we know that working together applies to students as well as teachers, we need to study how technology can contribute to this and how we can have an impact through communities to address world problems. Networking has been crucial to the success of all the projects I have ever founded.

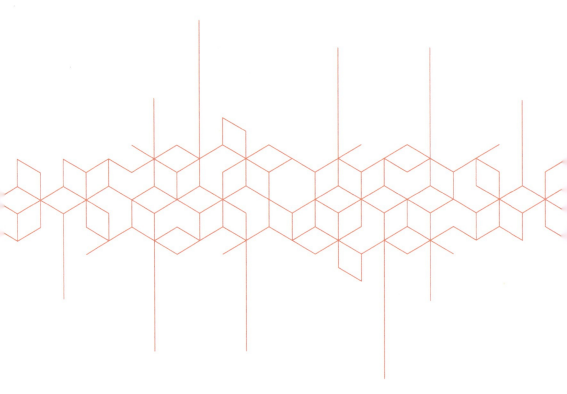

THE POWER OF COLLABORATION

6 REINFORCING LEARNING THROUGH TECHNOLOGY

Technology is rarely built specifically for education. It is usually created for business (PowerPoint), entertainment (Minecraft) or personal use (e-mail). Teachers then scramble to find useful tools for the classroom. And that is often quite a challenge.

I have always been very interested in using technology in education. Instead of writing a thesis to complete my teacher training, I embraced the option of developing a tool. In the preceding years, we used a thick book to discover which tree belongs to a leaf. This involved checking various traits of the leaf against various pages in a herbarium. This is called determining. I developed a tool that makes this much easier: the 'Interactive Determination Table'. After a few clicks on the screen - there were no smartphones yet - you discovered the name of the tree, its medicinal values and what the wood was used for. You can find the application on bomendetermineren.be. It is with this educational software that I won the trip to South Africa. It was in the final year of teacher training that I also discovered the internet. There was one computer on the entire campus that allowed you to surf to websites. While I was interested in the possibilities of being able to access an unlimited range of information, I was interested in one thing above all: how to build my own website. And just that question no lecturer could answer.

During the following years, I managed to create several websites. I also wrote educational manuals and ran into limitations: the books could not be in colour; when there was a mistake, a reprint was necessary; paper books do not allow animation and video. Now what if you offered textbooks online, within the context of an optimized self-learning course? Where regular updates are possible? A course with animations, colour and videos? In 2006, I developed zelfstudie.be. On this website, I offered all my courses that I had previously developed for my students in the classroom. The biggest differentiator was that students could choose between two formulas: a course with or without author support. That way, students could learn to build websites, work with PowerPoint, develop games and apps. But they could also develop web shops, work with MS Office and many other tools. Prices were deliberately kept low. For 10 euros, the price of a book, students could start learning. I learnt some things through the feedback I received. For instance, most students ordered support, but only an absolute minority actually asked questions. Because the courses are very hands-on, students were able to create their own website, document, shop or edited photos in no time. I also learnt that for some, learning from a screen is a barrier. Over the years, this began to become more and more of a habit for people. With the advent of smartphones, access to websites is at one's fingertips, allowing people to suddenly learn on the tram, at the beach and in a cafe. Mobile learning, as it is called, allows learning in less formal circumstances. And that is going to positively affect the learning process. The website would grow into the largest online school during the following years, with 28 000 students. Technology has the potential to add value to pupils' learning and teacher-designed tasks. Let us study how.

In 1951, US author Isaac Asimov wrote a science fiction story for children entitled *The Fun They Had*. The story is about two children who are taught at home by a computer that looks like a robot. It describes how this robot gives instructions and how much the children enjoy their learning. The first home computers did not appear until the 1980s.

Today, in many continents, technology is also starting to make its way into the classroom. Digital boards, laptops, tablets, beamers and tools that help with visualisation, examination, communication, feedback, organisation, collaboration, brainstorming, exploration and so on. But technology should not become uniformity. Sometimes it can make a big difference to students' learning, sometimes it is a gadget. Sometimes it is still the only option for offering education. So how do you know when it is valuable and how can you evaluate it? Let's start by distinguishing between technology and ICT. Technology includes a computer, a screen, a smartphone, a camera and a board. It includes ICT by which we mean software, apps and websites.

TPACK: successful integration of technology in teaching

In 2009, Bridge International Academies saw the light of day and profiled itself as 'the Uber of education'. With financial support from Bill Gates and Mark Zuckerberg, the idea to provide free education to children in underprivileged and often remote regions took shape. Schools were built in India, Kenya, Liberia, Nigeria and Uganda, and teachers were given a tablet with a script that meticulously describes the course of each lesson. Each teacher is theoretically interchangeable, as lessons are read verbatim from a tablet with a script on it. 'Ask the question …', 'well done', 'let students take notes for 1 minute', 'pause'. At the top, a timer displays the remaining lesson time. The scripts are developed by a study centre in Boston, which also collects massive data (timing, scores) to improve the scripts. In doing so, it also rigorously evaluates teachers: do they make eye contact every five seconds? Is their finger movement on the tablet screen fast enough? There isn't really time for questions. The intentions are good: if a teacher needs to be replaced for some reason, it can be instant. However, this is a classic case of technology being directly linked to the lesson topic. And where the teacher is considered merely a conveyer of information.

But sometimes teachers also make this mistake without realising it. They hear about a new tool, website or app and decide to use it in their lesson. The right approach is for the teacher to first look for the right pedagogical method and only then make a technological choice. The TPACK model by Koehler and Mishra (2009) stands for Technological Pedagogical Content Knowledge. It is a theory for teachers that shows which steps they need to take to teach efficiently while using technology.

The starting point is the lesson topic. The teacher searches for the best pedagogical working form, so that students can learn optimally. Teaching, teaching conversation, self-study, demonstration, class discussion, group work, self-study, field trip: various options are at hand. You will see that not all teachers make the same choice. Sometimes combinations are possible. And sometimes teachers will realize that they have made an error of judgement and they therefore choose a different working form next time. Only when this choice has been made, the teachers will decide on whether and which technology will be used.

Suppose a teacher is teaching about traffic. He may choose to take a small field trip around town, demonstrate, quote the rules, initiate a class discussion about a possible accident or use a dangerous traffic situation as a starting situation. Some forms require more time, budget, preparation, capacity and so on. These boundary factors can influence the teacher's choices, but it is crucial that the student's learning process is always at the centre.

The teaching method chosen will determine the technology required. For example, an excursion will require a camera, group work will require a browser and PowerPoint, demonstration may require Lego, and class discussion will not require any technology at all.

A prerequisite for this, however, is that the teacher is aware of the existing technologies. Those who do not know what is out there will also be unable to make informed decisions or will even avoid technology altogether. A great starting point to learn more about technologies with a great educational value is Jane Hart's annual top 200. You can find them at toptools4learning.com.

A teacher should also never assume that all features of technologies will reach their full potential in a classroom. Just because a tool enables certain scenarios does not mean it will effectively make them happen.

Belgian students learn about coral reefs with cheap VR glasses

For instance, I had been teaching via video conferencing tools (Zoom, MS Teams, Google Meet) in adult education for ten years before this approach was picked up during the COVID-19 pandemic out of necessity. The average age of my trainees was 50 and they learnt to build websites during my classes. Everyone's microphone and webcam were on, so everyone could ask questions at any time and engagement was optimal. However, because of the pandemic, I also suddenly had to teach in another group via Zoom: eighteen-year-old future teachers studying at Hogeschool PXL. Here we noticed a strange phenomenon: the students all very much chose not to use their microphone, but to communicate purely via chat. The webcam was not activated either. Only when instructed to use the microphone did they do so. The peripheral factors determined that some technological features did not come into their own: some students were not comfortable in their own skin; lessons were recorded and students wanted to avoid giving incorrect answers in this recording; some students wanted to guard their privacy as they were often forced to attend the class in their personal lives (room with posters, bed, small living space, outdated kitchen, and so on); some felt that an advantage of distance learning was that impeccable looks (clothes, make-up, and so on) were no longer required; others did register but did not really attend the class.

Thus, a teacher should never assume that conditions are optimal and therefore technology can be used optimally. In addition, of course, technology must also be available.

SAMR: evaluating the added value of technology

If you use technology in education, you should also be able to judge objectively how valuable it is. Puentedura's (2006) SAMR framework is interesting in this regard. SAMR is an acronym for *Substitution, Augmentation, Modification* and *Redefinition*. The model describes four possibilities. In the first phase, *substitution*, technology is deployed as a substitute tool. This phase is the weakest possible use of technology in education because the technology does not add value. Some examples: replace textbooks with iPads, use Google Maps instead of an atlas, use MS Word instead of a typewriter or apply Padlet instead of yellow sticky notes.

In the second phase, *augmentation,* there is already added value. Here, technology is used as a substitute tool and provides a functional improvement. For example,

MS Word indicating grammatical errors, Google Maps allowing to measure the distance between two cities, or the iPad having a search function.

Both phases, Substitution and Augmentation, provide convenience. But the pedagogy itself remain unchanged. There is nothing wrong with that, although it is questionable whether and to what extent the use of ICT at these levels effectively produces better learning outcomes. In any case, it does not deliver the transformation that many proponents hope for.

More can be expected from the third stage: *Modification*. Here, technology leads to an improvement in learning activity. Using MS Word online, for example, allows learners to collaborate. This implies that a teacher may decide not to correct articles submitted by the students themselves, but to let the students assess each other's work. That way, they learn from each other and give each other feedback. Only afterwards, the teacher corrects the original article and the other students' feedback. In this way, the pedagogy change.

Finally, there is the last phase, the one you should expect the most from: *Redefinition*. This is where technology is used in a transformative way in a learning activity that would not have been possible without the app or digital application. An example: thanks to Zoom and MS Teams, you can have a cross-cultural exchange with classes in other countries, or bring experts into the classroom.

The phases of Modification and Redefinition go far beyond Substitution and Augmentation. They have an impact on pedagogy. Pedagogy transforms, with the features of ICT leading to a redesign of learning activities or even to learning activities that were not possible without it. The added value of technology is ideally more than increased convenience, but leads to new pedagogical applications and much added value to the learning process: strong insights, collaboration and so on.

The SAMR model gives teachers an objective means by which they can assess whether the use of technology in their classroom adds value to their students' learning. In addition, it allows them to find out which technologies are merely gadgets. For example, schools that boast of being a 'tablet school', whether or not with the best of intentions or for marketing purposes. However, when the tablet simply replaces the paper textbook, it is doubtful whether there are any learning benefits for pupils; the tablet use is stuck in the first phase. But when pupils find information more quickly thanks to the tablet (search function), you get into the second phase. The tablet can only have a real transformative role when pupils enter the two subsequent phases.

The determination table I once developed will not drastically change the learning process. At most, it will speed up the search. Zelfstudie.be allows you to learn differently. Anytime, anywhere. But as far as the Climate Action Project is concerned, students and teachers worldwide can learn from each other, collaborate and show impact through technology. These applications correspond to the highest category.

Trend or gadget?

During an online meeting, I talk to Esther Wojcicki. Esther points out that we once relied on libraries and lost a lot of time looking up information there. And that the era we live in now, where technology has drastically changed some things, also requires a different kind of education (Wojcicki, 2019). Esther herself was a passionate teacher of journalism and ardent supporter of PBL before she retired. She is also the mother of YouTube's CEO. She mentions that every single day one billion searches in relation to educational resources are done on YouTube.

My friend Christian Williams has been teaching in Australia for decades. He was a gifted top lacrosse player. Unfortunately, due to heart failure, he did not make it to the Olympics. But he did not give up and found out which Olympic sports he could still do considering his heart condition. He taught himself archery, hammer throwing and bobsleigh by watching videos on YouTube and perfected his technique that way. He found a coach to help him with this, but who unfortunately spoke Japanese. He also learnt to speak that language with the help of technology.

Technology makes it possible to learn informally by browsing Wikipedia, looking for solutions on forums or exploring screencasts. Many of my friends taught themselves DIY, cooking or website creation by watching screencasts. Others learn by keeping an eye on posts from their Twitter network and become inspired. This is called accidental learning. In turn, colleague Koen revealed that he uses TikTok to watch short tutorials on MS Office. Knowing that our working memory has only seven places, *chunking* is an interesting way to learn: you break down information into smaller chunks. TikTok allows you to consume these short chunks. And no, not through dance performances.

Some technologies once amazed me, but when push came to shove, I never used them. Take speech technology in the car. The *EDUCAUSE Horizon Report, Teaching and Learning Edition* gives a nice annual overview of trends around technology in education. From artificial intelligence (AI) to hybrid learning, learning analytics and Open Educational Resources (OER) to micro-credentialing, you get a nice insight into how they predict technology will take hold in education in the near future.

Gamification and game-based learning

Why are students not always motivated when given a difficult task in class and why do they persevere when playing a video game? That is the question James Gee (2011) asked himself. He started studying why young people do persevere when they reach a difficult level in a game and started weaving elements from games into the learning process. The terms *gamification* and *game-based learning* are often mixed up.

Gamification means taking the rewarding elements from a game and weaving them into the lesson: badges and levels to reward, credits, an avatar that can be personalised, or quests where a next chapter only unlocks when you achieve a goal. The focus is on game elements that reward and reinforce engagement in the learning process.

In *game-based learning*, you use the game itself in the lesson to support critical thinking and problem-solving. These games are often called 'serious games'. People often use Second Life and Minecraft. The focus is on the game itself, which is used to deliver learning materials in an engaging way.

Lego bricks used to teach fractions or traffic situations, Minecraft used to visualise 3D views or having students build a hospital while speaking another language: using games in class allows you to transform on the SAMR scale and promote collaboration, mainly in a constructivist way. They can be used both synchronously and asynchronously. It is invariably a task I give to my students in teacher training. When I was in a panel discussion with an American professor in Dubai, she described gamification as the flavour given to bad-tasting medicines, openly questioning

A Minecraft world that makes sea levels rise if students do not take the necessary actions

whether this should be necessary for learning, which should be inherently inviting. And she has a point. But video games and certain factors can certainly support some pedagogical working forms and enable new situations. During the Climate Action Project, US teacher Joe Fatheree thought that making one big virtual world might lead to a nice result. He invited pupils from 50 different countries to all work together to build a sustainable world. Students from Hawaii to New Zealand built solar panels, wind turbines, green buildings and even a real hyperloop. At any time of the day, someone was working in the virtual world. At the same time, Lego was often used to give students insights. For example, sustainable alternatives for transport, travel and food were important too. Richard himself created his own Minecraft world with a story. For example, you need to build solar panels and windmills to stop rising sea levels. But then the villagers get nervous because the sea view is blurred. At the end of the game, you get a score for skills such as problem-solving, creativity and empathy.

Wearables: learning with VR and AR

'Wearables' are devices you can wear. They can be items of clothing, accessories such as a bracelet, watch or glasses, or even implants. The best-known wearables are virtual reality (VR) and augmented reality (AR) glasses.

You could say that smartwatches and AR glasses are the extension of a smartphone. They often have the same capabilities: audio recording or quickly looking something up via the smartwatch, emails or consulting the GPS as an enhancement on the AR glasses. Shadiev et al. (2018) used smartwatches to provide feedback to students learning English to help them learn the correct pronunciation of words.

What is the difference between virtual reality and augmented reality? With VR, you watch through glasses and see nothing of your surroundings. With AR, you watch through a pair of glasses or a smartphone and, in the process, your environment is enriched with *additional* information. With AR glasses, you can watch an instructional video while attending class, open your mailbox against a wall, study 3D models of body parts or place name tags above your students' heads. But apps on a smartphone or tablet also make AR possible: looking through your smartphone, you can place a volcano or a skeleton on a table or in the corner of the classroom. As the term suggests, AR enriches your environment.

With VR, there are two versions: low-end and high-end. Low-end glasses require you to plug in your smartphone. These glasses are also called *cardboard*, after the cheap cardboard Google glasses. The high-end glasses include a computer and controllers and are easily a hundred times more expensive. Clever VR tools take you to the *Mona Lisa* in the Louvre or sloths in Costa Rica. Minocha et al. (2018) used VR in geography to take students on a virtual trip to Australian coral reefs. Fabola and Miller (2016) used VR in history to take students to Saint Andrew's Cathedral in the fourteenth century.

Thanks to AR, you can better visualise complex concepts, access information faster and teach procedures. In turn, using the AR tool Layar, you can conjure up videos, animations and extra info on textbooks. Both VR and AR allow information to be enriched and displayed more clearly. Students can gain better insights and it can also bring practical benefits.

Belgian teacher Olivier Dijkmans uses cheap VR glasses with Google Expeditions, allowing his students to travel to places that would be unfeasible for real field trips. That way, they see the impact climate change is having on our environment. But they also get to know the places where students with whom they have had a virtual exchange live. Other teachers use free AR apps on their smartphones to place a tsunami model or tornado on the table so that those phenomena can be studied in detail.

Artificial intelligence (AI): the chatbot

Personally, I think AI has the potential to be profound in terms of technological innovation. But what can it mean for education?

AI is the ability of a system to correctly interpret external data, learn from it, and use these lessons to achieve specific goals and tasks through flexible adaptation (Haenlein and Kaplan, 2019). But it is a broad term, as there are many applications. An interesting one that captures the imagination is the chatbot. You often come across a chatbot on the website of larger online shops. It is technology that answers automatically, based on information found on websites, in older mail conversations or other sources. In 1966, Joseph Weizenbaum built the first chatbot, called Eliza. He did so in just 120 lines and considered his creation more of a gadget. The relational chatbot could conduct conversations, engaging in pattern matching and repeating a user's words to increase engagement. When Weizenbaum asked his secretary to give Eliza a test run, she asked him to leave the room after only 30 minutes because the conversation was getting too personal. You can test the bot yourself on this website: masswerk.at/elizabot.

I also once developed a chatbot in order to be able to answer questions that come back very often. The process is quite time-intensive, as the bot needs to be initially trained and fed information. But the thing is available around the clock and can offer more targeted information than search engines. Since I need to feed the chatbot myself, you cannot talk about AI. With ChatGPT and Bard, you can.

When ChatGPT was launched, social media were swamped by opinion makers who all wanted to show how it would impact their jobs. ChatGPT is generative AI for creating text, images, music and even video. You can ask questions to ChatGPT to then get a summary of a book, a commentary on a famous person, a recipe or a business plan within seconds. But the clever part is that you can start a real conversation. Whereas in Google you always have to start over by asking questions, here you can build on your search. You can have daily posts drafted for your social media, you can also ask them to generate a piece of code or, on the contrary, have them find a bug in your own code. This development makes us think about how quickly a search engine like Google, which dominated the market for more than a decade, can become irrelevant and a global company can suddenly thunder out of the top ten. But ChatGPT also generates wrong answers. And we need to teach our teachers and students to deal with that. In this regard, you can reflect on whether you still need to do a job that ChatGPT can already take over. After all, the chatbot can offer more than just information. It also allows you to create things. For instance, little brother Dall-E can generate pictures. A painting of an astronaut on a horse in pastel shades? A photorealistic image of a classroom of the future? It can do it all. The first reaction was related to plagiarism and how to avoid this from now on. And through ElevenLabs' IIEI, you can clone a voice and have everything read out through your own voice.

I am in a meeting with Ross. He has worked at Microsoft for decades, but I especially know him from a walk we took in Brussels. Since then, we have had one meeting a year. It was also Ross who introduced me to the Fellowship of the British Royal Society of Arts. Since then, I have been allowed to claim the prestigious title of FRSA, just as Stephen Hawking, Marie Curie and Nelson Mandela. Ross is currently working on a PhD on ethical algorithms for AI and argues that it is only waiting for AI to learn from itself.

But the real question is how to adapt our education to a situation where there is a new source of information. For instance, the pocket calculator and Google Translate have not made education irrelevant either. And that brings us to the next issue.

Why memorise facts when you have Google?

Now that we know that technology can have quite some positive impact on learning, the question arises: why do we still need to memorise facts when we have Google?

I once took part in a panel in Dubai where two teams of two took different positions on a proposition. Ours was 'Is "I can just Google it" making us stupid?'. Unfortunately, I couldn't choose which camp I was in - that's how it goes with conferences - but that didn't make the debate any less fervent.

Adherents of connectivism sometimes go so far as to say that it no longer makes any sense at all for young people to have to memorise the world's capital cities for exams if they can quickly find this information on Google after leaving the classroom. It is like arguing that you no longer need to know grammar rules because a word processor will point out the mistakes.

An important mistake is made here: there is a big difference between information and knowledge. Information is found on websites, in books or if you listen to a teacher. Knowledge, on the other hand, is processed information in your head. A brain has given meaning to that information. And it is precisely this knowledge that enables learners to develop intellectually. So we should not outsource our memory. To put it very succinctly, we still want doctors who can make an informed diagnosis and pilots who make correct decisions during emergency scenarios without having to turn to Google to do so.

Ray Kurzweil (2005) argues that in the near future we will be able to link the human brain with the cloud. Kurzweil is known for his accurate predictions. In the 1990s, for instance, he predicted that by 2009, electronic screens would be integrated into glasses, cables would have largely disappeared and we would mainly use mobile computers. In addition, he is the inventor of the scanner and headed AI at Google. Elon Musk is also toying with this idea. An interesting fact. But do they mean that the information - and not knowledge - on the internet becomes accessible to the brain or that the knowledge already in the brain becomes available in the cloud? In either scenario, this seems problematic. Kurzweil also wrote about singularity, arguing that technological evolution is exponential, and that computers will soon become super-intelligent and overtake human intelligence. For instance, Kurzweil predicts that computers will exceed the brain capacity of a person in the near future. By 2045, they would even reach the equivalent of the brains of all humans combined. Earlier, Bill Gates, Stephen Hawking and Elon Musk warned against artificial intelligence for this reason. They fear that AI cannot be controlled, should it fall into the hands of world leaders with wrong intentions, or robots.

Resistance to technology

The English weaver Ned Ludd saw a danger in machines and destroyed two weaving machines in 1779. Around him gathered a movement of artisans and small farmers who saw a threat in industrial and technological developments. *Luddism* was born. Resistance to innovation is of all centuries. Socrates saw an enemy of memory in the written word. In China, people continued to use papyrus for a long time because they considered paper a dangerous innovation, and in the 1950s there was a real resistance to the ballpoint pen.

For teachers, too, the use of technology can come across as overwhelming and intrusive. Sometimes this is accompanied by resistance. During the COVID-19 pandemic, two requirements turned out to be very important: teachers need to be properly trained so that they can handle technology. In addition, they need to understand the importance of pedagogy and technology and become aware of the latter's potential. So that its benefits and direct impact on students' learning process become clear.

Five tips to tackle resistance to technology:

1. Give teachers enough time.
2. Appreciate the teacher's ideas.
3. Put the teacher at the wheel.
4. Opt for bottom-up, start from the workplace.
5. Start small and sweet.

So when you want to introduce technology to teachers or in a school, you should always do so thoughtfully. Since the Climate Action Project relies heavily on technology, this means we mainly have participants who are willing to use technology during their lessons.

Conclusion

Technology is rarely developed for education, and consequently teachers look for ways to create added value to their lessons themselves. Research shows that young people today still mainly use technology to consume information rather than cre-

REINFORCING LEARNING THROUGH TECHNOLOGY

Canadian students use the green screen to act out scenarios

ate (Tan, 2014). Technology is helping to empower and even transform education. It has the potential to make a difference during lessons and thus it has a positive impact on a student's learning process. However, in doing so, the teacher must always focus on the pedagogical method first and be able to distinguish between technology that has the potential to transform on the one hand and mere gadgets on the other. For this, he must be aware of the technology available. To use technology correctly in distance learning, you need to make the right choice between synchronous and asynchronous teaching.

Will technology ever make memory obsolete? Possibly not. After all, there is a difference between information and knowledge. But technology also makes it possible to collaborate, even globally. It is especially here that transformations can be made. Let us examine further how we can use technology to create a real movement and tackle world problems through a project.

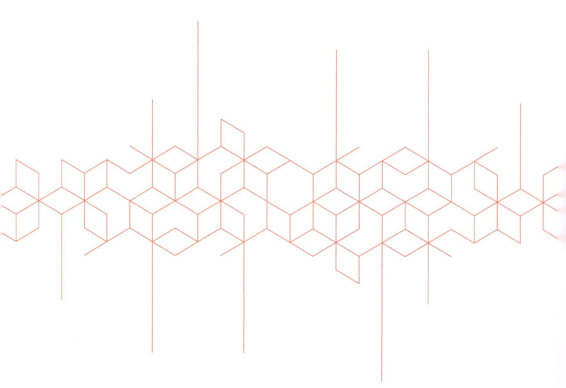

REINFORCING LEARNING THROUGH TECHNOLOGY

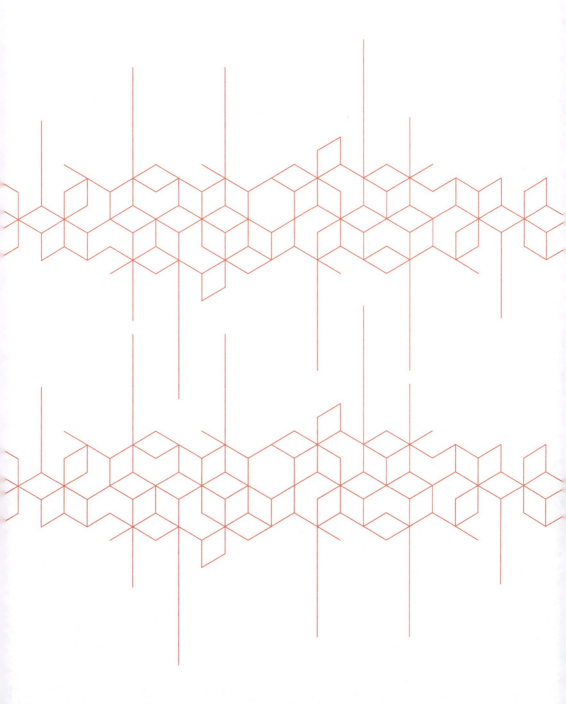

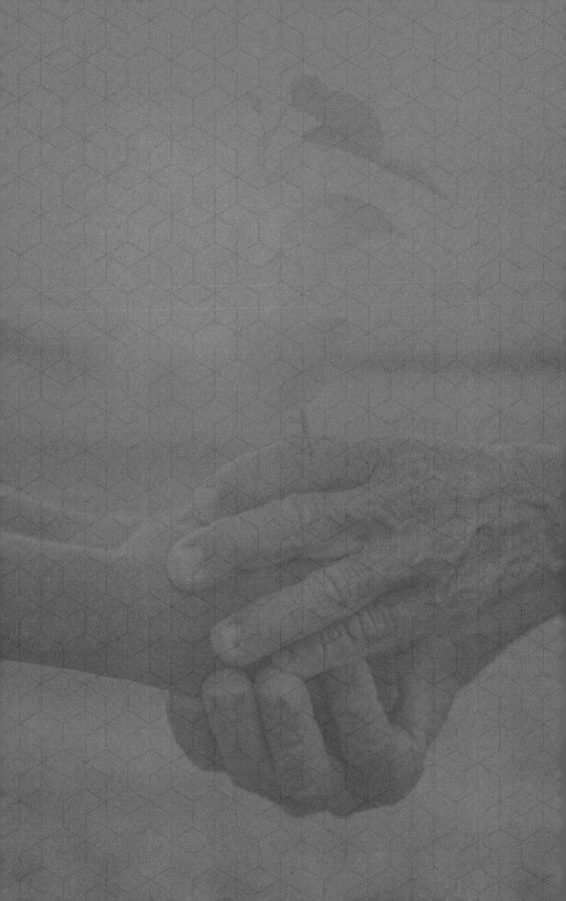

7 BEHAVIOUR CHANGE AND MINDSET

Individual responsibility

The 2022 IPCC report argues that changing behaviour and lifestyle can reduce global CO_2 emissions from humans in a short time. The IPCC is the Intergovernmental Panel on Climate Change, a United Nations organisation established to assess the risks of climate change. The IPCC states that by implementing the right policies and providing the infrastructure and technology, we can reduce emissions by 40-70% by 2050 through behavioural change (Pörtner, 2022).

Although 92% of Europeans now agree that greenhouse gas emissions need to be reduced (European Commission, 2019), there has not yet been the large-scale behavioural change that is nevertheless required to keep the average temperature on earth from rising dangerously. Support seems to be growing, yet it is not yet embraced en masse. How can that be? When people see fire and feel heat, they instinctively move to safety. But we cannot perceive the threat of global warming with our senses. It is abstract and many people do not see and feel the consequences. Not now, not here and not in their personal situation. This psychological distance in time, space and socially lowers people's motivation to take action (Trope and Liberman, 2010). Once they feel psychologically closer to the consequences of climate change, people tend to be more engaged and more willing to take actions to combat climate change (Spence, Poortinga & Pidgeon, 2012). The extent to which people are motivated for environmentally friendly behaviour is partly determined by the extent to which people find it meaningful. This has to do with the values that are important to them (Steg, Perlaviciute & van der Werff, 2015). For example, people who value doing something for others and for nature are more motivated to behave in an environmentally friendly way.

There are several psychological factors that actually get people to do something for the climate. For example, people are more likely to effectively take action if they are really concerned (Bouman et al., 2020). In climate education, it is important not to throw young people into climate anxiety, but of course they should know the facts. Different age groups can also handle a different dose of reality in this regard. In addition, people need a clear action perspective that is achievable (Michie, 2018) and need to be confident that the actions they take are part of the solution and will make a real difference (Samaddar et al., 2014). Thus, not only small, manageable actions will need to be shown to students during lessons, but at the same time their impact on their immediate environment.

Stern (2000) argues that there are five types of climate-relevant actions, which are important for a transition to a sustainable society: climate activism (participating in demonstrations), non-activist behaviour in a public sphere (signing petitions and supporting climate policies), climate behaviour in the private sphere (consumer behaviour), climate behaviour in the work environment (sustainable choices made by entrepreneurs) and collective climate action (whole villages committed to a sustainable place).

In general, the following is true for all climate-relevant action: before people take action, they must be sufficiently motivated to do it, have the capacity to do it, and be given the opportunity to do it (Michie et al., 2018). The Climate Action Project tries to address this by creating the opportunity and capacity, and fostering motivation during the process.

To promote behavioural change, it is also important to make sustainable behaviour the norm. Today, solar panels, electric cars and organic food still cost more than the more polluting alternatives. Making climate education a standard part of the curriculum will drastically lower the threshold to participate and thereby obtain a behavioural change.

People should also feel that it is socially desirable to change their behaviour. Especially when they see others doing the same, it will have an impact on their behaviour (Cialdini, 2007). When those others have a high status or are just very similar to them, they are even more likely to join in. It is especially pernicious if they feel they are on their own (Michie, 2018). During the Climate Action Project, students worldwide show each other what actions they are taking. In the process, messages are shared about what behaviour is undesirable. Students are encouraged by each other, but also through the video messages of experts and public figures.

Finally, in desired behavioural change it is important that people feel that the distribution of costs is done in an equitable way, following a proper procedure (Bleijenberg et al., 2020). Or, when they are shaken out of their routine, or there is a clearly defined moment when climate-friendly action is actually made possible (Verplanken and Roy, 2016). In the case of the Climate Action Project, we clearly see Climate Action Day as this moment.

Mindset

Apart from an individual responsibility we bear, which requires behavioural change, teachers must also feel that they can address climate change or other world problems in their classrooms. What is required for teachers to participate in the Climate Action Project?

When I was seventeen, I had a very big problem speaking English. I couldn't get an English word past my lips. The fear of failure was too great. Even when the teacher mentioned that you could not pass that year if you had not participated in the conversation at least once. At 33, I decided to start a master's degree in Sheffield: Technology Enhanced Learning, Innovation and Change. I could complete the training remotely, but to do so I had to convince a professor that my English was adequate. With great difficulty, I wrote a text that I then memorised. The morning of the interview, I felt miserable and almost cancelled the interview.

Seven years later, I step confidently onto the stage in Abu Dhabi. I am speaking there at the invitation of the royal family. Earlier, I spoke in London, Paris, Washington, Beijing and Moscow. I notice a TV studio built in the conference room. Nothing is impossible in the United Arab Emirates. I approach the director of Abu Dhabi TV and ask if they are interested in my story. An hour later, I go live under very strange circumstances. The two presenters ask me a question in Arabic. Behind the scenes is a translator who whispers the translation into English to me through an earpiece. Only ... he doesn't speak the language himself. With every second of silence, I see the presenters becoming more uncomfortable. Although the translator is still in the middle of his sentence, I take off to explain the essence of the Climate Action Project. Wide-eyed, I see the presenters stare at me. That evening, I board a plane. The crew come to greet me one by one and announce that my return flight is under the patronage of the royal family. This time, I see the people around me staring wide-eyed. Before I doze off, I wonder how it is possible that decades earlier I could not utter a word of English and today I found myself live on TV on another continent. Later, I discovered the answer: I had a fixed mindset.

Why do some students persevere when the going gets tough, while others quickly give up? According to Carol Dweck (2008), people have either a fixed or a growth mindset. People with a fixed mindset assume that personality and intelligence are more or less fixed. They believe that you are born with a certain intelligence. And in this way, they sometimes even grow a sense of inferiority. I myself assumed that I would never be able to speak and learn English. People with a growth mindset assume that you can change everything gradually. They believe you can get smarter through practice. Therefore, they try longer when something fails. They look ahead and try to learn lessons from mistakes. The difference in mindset often determines your life course and can be the key to gaining experiences, success and happiness.

Why do some people have a fixed mindset and others a growth mindset? According to Dweck, one of the factors is praising commitment. By encouraging students, you can drive them towards a growth mindset. Dweck shows that at the struggle and resistance stage, the main explanation for dropout lies in the fact that each learner deals with frustration differently. Those who have had some successes are also more likely to have a growth mindset because they want to protect this status.

It is crucial for the Climate Action Project that pupils feel that their contribution adds to cooperation. To support this, the teacher must guide pupils in the best possible way. But the teacher also needs a growth mindset to participate in a project that often requires them to take a big step out of their comfort zone because both the topic and the pedagogical approach are unexplored.

What drives people?

As an eighteen-year-old, you are searching for your identity. I clearly remember having interesting conversations with my friend Paul in his attic room. One of them is still very fresh in my memory. It was about Thomas Hobbes, who argued that people always act for their own benefit and so, by definition, are actually egoists (Gert, 1967). So what about giving gifts to others or taking care of your children? According to Hobbes, you also do this because it gives you satisfaction and thus in turn contributes to your own benefit and well-being. It is a proposition you should let dormant and you don't need to agree with. After all, that's how it goes in philosophy. But it remains an interesting thought. But what drives people to participate in the Climate Action Project and perhaps even go the 'extra mile'?

There are several reasons from an intrinsic motivation why teachers wish to participate: they care about the climate, they want to learn from each other in an international project, they are hungry for a new experience in their career, they want to be part of a bigger picture, they want to offer opportunities to their students or they need a certificate to gain continuing education points.

There are also bold participants who do participate for the badge and the photo they can share on social media. But by offering quality and good support, we can nurture intrinsic motivation. Although that badge too has its role, I will learn later.

Maslow

Finally, we need to reflect on cultural diversity, which is often ignored in research. Maslow is famous for his pyramid of needs, which visualises human needs. These go from physiological needs (eating, breathing, sleeping) to security (safety, protection, health), social acceptance (love, friendship), esteem (success, respect) and self-fulfilment (creativity, study, ethics). Only when the basic needs are met can you move to the next need. As far as the Climate Action Project is concerned, it is a confronting reality that teachers and students who cannot meet their basic needs will not be that inclined to take climate action or participate in the project. Yet, we see passionate people living in very challenging circumstances participating out of great conviction. Their regions are struggling with harvest and livestock losses and they see severe floods threatening their homes. It is not as natural for every teacher to invest time in the Climate Action Project.

Conclusion

Refugees, climate change, gender inequality, poverty: these are not small issues. Young people may already have a certain point of view, shaped by their upbringing, experiences, the media. What do we want to achieve through education? Pupils need to be presented with the right knowledge, along with important skills. But tackling world problems requires a change in behaviour and mindset.

If we ask students to take action, it will only succeed in the long run if there is intrinsic motivation and if we encourage them to do so and make them see the importance of their actions. We can do this by offering them authentic experiences and leaving them free to discover things for themselves and find solutions. It is important that pupils realise that they have the capabilities to do so. They go through various stages where they may not see the problem at first, resist for a while, but finally take action.

But the cultural factor also plays a role. Can you ask a child who has no food to recycle or care about the climate?

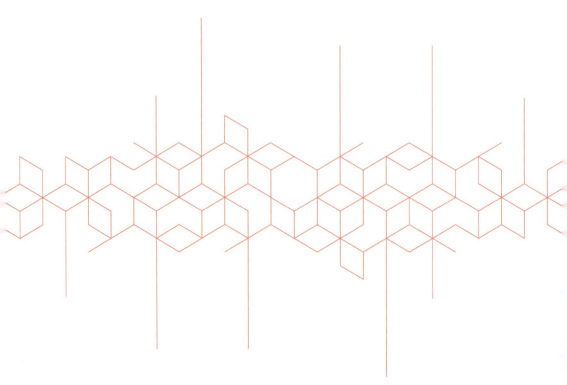

BEHAVIOUR CHANGE AND MINDSET

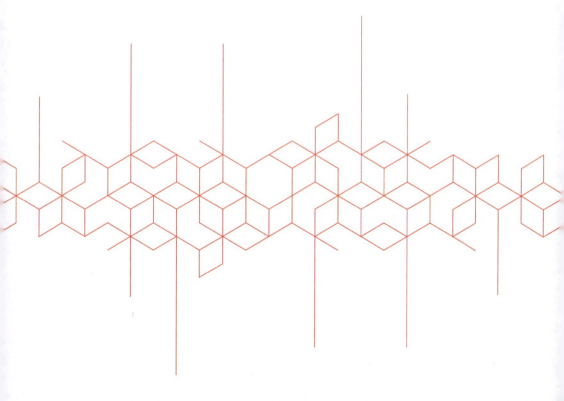

8 THE IMAGE PROBLEM OF CLIMATE CHANGE

Climate change. Some people ignore it. Others try with heart and soul to do something about it. Many people react vigorously. However, there are also still a lot of people who know almost nothing about the problem.

First, we focus on the phenomenon of climate change. Then we look for the best way to communicate about it.

Climate

Some of the headlines: in California, the largest forest fire in the state's history is raging, Antarctica records a heat record of 5.6 degrees Celsius, in Pakistan, birds fall dead from the sky in temperatures of 50 degrees Celsius, and in northern Greenland, there was a heat wave that melted 18 billion tonnes of ice in as little as three days.

There is a famous meme featuring Homer and Bart Simpson. In it, Bart complains: 'This is the hottest summer of my life.' To which Homer replies: 'It's the coldest summer of the rest of your life.' Meet climate change. Immense forest fires, floods, tornadoes, crop failures, scorching heat waves, and dry riverbeds are some of the many consequences. Climatologist Wim Thiery indicates that if we compare the average temperature of the last 20 years with the beginning of the industrial period, we are now at a warming of 1 degree. And each decade adds 0.2 degrees.

The big problem is that 1.5 degrees doesn't sound like an extreme amount to most people. But imagine your body temperature rising from 37 degrees to 38.5 degrees: then you have a problem. At the UN climate conference in Paris in 2015, it was agreed to limit warming to well below 2 degrees, preferably 1.5 degrees. In 2022, the UN climate panel calculated that it will rather be 2.4 degrees. In that scenario, children born in 2020 will experience 37 times more heat waves than the generation born in 1960. Added to this, by the end of the century there will be twice as many forest fires, twice as many tropical cyclones, three times as many floods, four times as many crop failures, six times as many droughts and 37 times more heat waves than in a world without climate change. You can make the calculation yourself at myclimatefuture.info.

Fact: a Boeing 747 consumes about 100 tonnes of fossil fuels on a flight from London to Hong Kong. One percent of the world's population flies a lot; they account for half of the aviation pollution. The carbon budget is the amount of CO_2 we can burn while still staying below a certain level of warming, in order to stay below 1.5 degrees by 2030 (Hsu, 2014). This budget is between 200 and 300 billion tonnes of CO_2. We emit some 40 billion tonnes of CO_2 per year, so our budget will run out between 2026 and 2042.

The solution

Our current world population is 7.7 billion people. It is only a fraction of the 100 billion people who once lived and a sneeze compared to the 6.75 trillion (6.750.000.000.000) people who will live during the next fifty thousand years. Roman Krznaric (2020) argues that we have colonised our future and wonders what we will leave them. According to him, the power lies in large groups of people decolonising the future thanks to sustainable actions. Zaval et al. (2015) confirm and argue that people are open to behavioural change when their actions in the now are linked to their legacy. How they are thought of by others later and whether they leave the world better for future generations.

There are two solutions to stop or even reverse climate change: climate adaptation and climate mitigation. The difference between the two is that mitigation will address the causes and minimise the impact. Adaptation, on the other hand, focuses mainly on impacts, reduces negative effects, and tries to find opportunities.

Climate adaptation is the process by which societies reduce their vulnerability to climate change or take advantage of the opportunities presented by a changing climate. Adaptation policies are still in their infancy in many countries. Examples include: protecting people from floods by building houses in higher areas, planting trees, adapting infrastructure, providing assistance to vulnerable groups in the population and drawing up plans to prevent disaster scenarios, roller skating instead of skating in winter, collecting rainwater for use during droughts.

Climate mitigation (Fisher, 2007) consists of measures intended to reduce the extent or rate of global warming. Generally, the term means reducing man-made emissions of greenhouse gases. In addition, mitigation can include increasing the capacity of carbon sinks, including through reforestation. Examples: use of green energy (solar panels, wind turbines), efficient energy use (lighting) and sustainable transport.

Climate education can consist of both options: adaptation and mitigation. For example, we think of training teachers, sensitising school leaders, adapting lessons, informing parents and activating young people while offering them the necessary insights and skills.

Communicating climate change

In the 1940s, top salesman Elmer Wheeler stated in *Time Magazine*: 'Don't sell the sausage - sell the sizzle.' His thesis: when you advertise, don't talk about the sausage, but about the sizzling sound, the tasty juices and the inviting smells, to make people hungry. We have been trying to sell climate change for years now, but many people don't buy it. And as a result, it has become a seller's problem, not a scientist's. Instead of banging our heads against a hard wall of climate deniers, we need to find our sizzle. After all, climate change is the sausage, and here comes a second metaphor: our message is often that we are going to hell. Rising sea levels, a scorched earth and dying climate refugees. Against all odds, however, hell does not sell a hissing sound. While the image of a burning earth may be accurate and eye-catching, it will not make people change their behaviour.

There is one message almost everyone responds positively to, though: the image of building a sky without dirty exhaust fumes.

Discussions on climate change are now also taking place in living rooms and on terraces. It will be people and not just world leaders who will make the difference. Without them changing their lifestyles, a fight against climate change does not stand a chance. And so we must speak to them. Without their support, the cynics win.

One simple roadmap makes this possible: start with a vision, give a choice, make a plan and move on to action. Time for some more explanation.

So an appropriate strategy to communicate about climate is to focus on heaven rather than hell. In one sentence, describe a future with few emissions. This captures the imagination and plays on emotions: hope, progress and excitement for tomorrow. The big problem with climate change messages is not that people don't agree or understand, but simply that they don't listen. So it has to be presented visually. You have to create an image of your message, which by the way should be local. Don't talk about forest fires in Australia if you want to convince people in South Africa. So you have to find out what your audience wants, respond to that and show how your vision will contribute to that. Data and statistics have no place here. Those are for action plans, not visions. 50% less CO_2 by 2030 is not a vision,

Nigerian students sharing images during a flood

but a goal. Put all the targets together and imagine what the world would be like. That is a vision.

Now that you have been introduced to heaven, you have to show hell. This will create the choice between two scenarios. It is crucial that you demonstrate that this is the time to make the choice. Therefore, you need to explain what you are trying to avoid.

Most people will now wonder what you are going to do to avoid this, so at this stage you must show your strong and simple plan. The public will only listen if you offer great, meaningful and memorable achievements. Do you know what 2050 will look like? That's still a long way off. Keep your plan for three to five years. Or even shorter, if you can make a difference in that time frame.

Finally, it's time for your question. Your story includes some specific actions people can take to turn us away from the potential danger. To ensure that the 21st century is better than the 20th. This is your question. Make it specific and clear and show how it will achieve the vision. Your language should match your audience. Limit yourself to actions that this audience can perform.

In his TED talk, John Marshall (2021) describes three strategies for communicating climate change effectively. He argues that a surprisingly high number of people have never heard of climate change and that only 25% of Americans are concerned about it. This is obviously absurd: something is very thoroughly wrong and people are puzzled by this situation. Marshall argues that we are failing to communicate about climate change.

The problem is that climate change is abstract, distant and too big to understand. We use terms like CO_2, net zero, emissions … which are confusing. They become obstacles and they don't help to understand the problem, let alone care about it. The solution is to see people as individuals and communicate in such a way that they care about climate change.

A first working point is speaking in a clear and universal language. That is, no scientific terms. Preventing global warming of 2 degrees? Two degrees, that doesn't sound so bad. 1.2 trillion tonnes of ice? That's so much that you don't even understand it. Confusion and helplessness are the enemy of understanding.

'The hole in the ozone layer' is much more comprehensible than 'climate change'. A hole can be easily imagined. Therefore, when it comes to climate change, we need to create a clear picture. This can be done as follows. We have lived on earth for 300.000 years and only during the last 60 years have we started polluting so fiercely. In the process, we create a thick blanket of pollution that traps heat in the atmosphere. This heat causes violent tornadoes, bigger fires, more floods and the extinction of thousands of species. To stop the 'pollution blanket', we simply have to stop polluting. This metaphor is well received and understood.

When delivering the message, you should also be clear. Instead of 'warming', say 'overheating' and replace 'climate' with 'extreme weather'. Irreversibility catches people's attention. The first step is to make your language understandable and relevant.

A second point is to make it relevant. Explain how your life will change because of climate change. No one is waiting for policy proposals. You don't tell people in Florida that we need zero emissions to stop climate change, you tell them 'stop the tornadoes', in Australia you say 'stop the forest fires' and in Sierra Leone 'stop the floods'. Every parent cares about this. So we are not talking about our future life, but our life. Not our children, but our child.

Finally, we need to communicate climate change as something that happens to all of us. People may care about their environment, but therefore may not feel affection for terms like 'environmentalist'. But they may already be doing good work.

That we learn from communicating about climate change also applies to messages about refugees, poverty, peace and gender inequality.

You turn it into a personal story that resonates with your audience, using understandable language and focusing on the positive. Because although the term 'refugee' has negative connotations for some, it is actually about someone who is forced to flee. Something that can happen to all of us.

Climate Visuals dedicates an entire website to photos you should use when talking about climate change (and which ones not at all). The polar bear on the ice floe touches the audience very little. Keep the following in mind: 1) show real people, not contrived stock photos; 2) tell new stories; 3) show climate change at scale; 4)

THE IMAGE PROBLEM OF CLIMATE CHANGE

The positive approach: children in Montenegro and their Planet Earth craft

respond to emotions; 5) understand your audience; 6) make it local; 7) be careful with photos about protest.

From communicating to teaching

I am preparing for an interview with the BBC. They are making a series on climate change and would like to ask me questions about climate education. For this interview, they use special software that captures the voice in the best possible way. By now, my family already knows that this means they'd better go outside for a while to ensure absolute silence. But that didn't apply to my neighbour, who thought it was about time to take his chainsaw off the shelf once more. I install myself at breakneck speed in my son's room, which borders the garden of a neighbour whose fingers are less green. I start the interview punctually at 11 o'clock, my knees almost touching my ears since my son's chair is several sizes too small. The host asks how we deal with 'climate anxiety', the fear that young people develop after all the doomsday reports about climate change. I answer her that it is important that students realise the seriousness, but that we then proceed with a positive approach. In the classroom there is no room for 'our house is on fire' and emaciated polar bears are not productive if you aim to change behaviour among students. Our project therefore focuses on solutions, small actions that everyone can take and which are required to move forward.

Education about sustainability is often associated with the head-heart-hands approach (Singleton, 2015). This is an approach with three main pillars: *hands* stand for active participation, *head* stands for knowledge and understanding about the topic, and *heart* for concern. Marshall Ganz (2010) argues that strategy and narrative lead to action. Under 'strategy' *(head)* he counts the how, analysis, reason; under 'story' *(heart)* he counts the why, feeling and motivation. Together, they lead to action *(hands)*.

Tilbury (1993) links this to three ways of setting up environmental education: about, in and for. *About* is linked to *head*. Teaching about sustainability and the environment raises awareness and increases knowledge and understanding about interactions between humans and the environment. This approach neglects political aspects. It is also a conservative way of offering education, with only little correlation between knowledge acquisition and actual action for, say, a better climate (UNESCO, 1986).

In is linked to *heart* and involves a learner-centred approach focused on problem solving. Here you work on raising awareness and concerns often arise automatically. This approach also neglects political aspects. If you were to use this approach exclusively, the risk of frustration, guilt and even anxiety grows (Coward, 1990). As a result, there is only a very limited share in bringing real change to the environment with this approach.

For is paired with *hand*. Hands-on teaching and learning create a sense of responsibility and active participation. This approach does not ignore political aspects. The approach is problem-oriented, promoting a sustainable lifestyle. Everyone is responsible for their own actions.

When I founded the project in 2017, I focused mostly on *heart* and *hand*. In doing so, I made the mistake of undervaluing knowledge. I argued that we need students who can find solutions, not just recite the definition of climate change. But I was wrong. Students need to be able to do both. Because if you don't know the definition, you can't take action either. Fien (1993) confirms and argues that all three pillars - *about*, *in* and *for* - must be involved in climate education to get the right knowledge, skills and motivation.

Sometimes you just need knowledge to modify your behaviour. Did you know that 65% of climate change caused by schools is due to food waste? Very often, just knowing facts is enough as a first step to adjust your behaviour. Don't waste food. Don't take more than you need. This does not even require investment. There are several ways to tackle or even reverse climate change. Education is one of them. But how exactly can you have a positive impact on the environment through education? Is it by giving our young people insights or encourage them to take action?

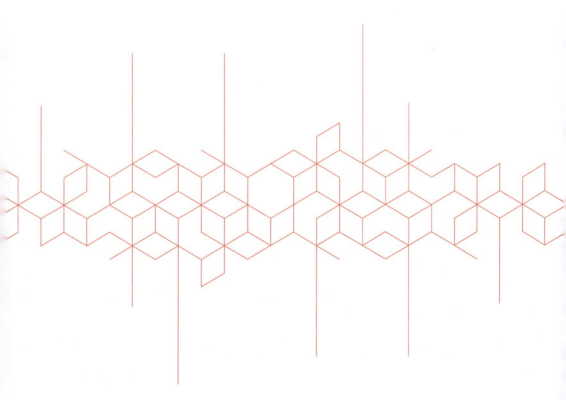

9 THE NEED FOR CLIMATE EDUCATION

In some regions young people are losing the connection with nature. They often no longer know the origin of some natural products. On the other hand, we hardly know what takes place under the smoke plumes of factories. We simply no longer know what processes precede the production of everyday things like cars, soft drinks and plastic. And certainly not what kind of pollution this involves. Sometimes it is enough to point something out to people. Many young people and adults do not know that - often cheap – purchases are container-shipped from another continent, or that a certain fruit variety is sometimes flown in from another country … resulting in a huge carbon footprint. While we should support each other globally, we should try to buy local.

If you know that glass never decays, you are less likely to throw it into nature. If you recognise that a plastic container that ends up in nature might end up in the ocean and then persist for hundreds of years in the form of tiny fibres coming out of people's taps, you will start behaving differently. That is more efficient than fining violations. When I worked out a curriculum for the new Rethink Plastic Project, I learnt a huge amount. Every single-use plastic item I touch now, I look at in a completely different way. Sometimes, we don't need real lesson plans, but clearly need to remind each other of the impact of our actions.

The problem is that teachers are often unsure about controversial topics and avoid talking about anything that might cause anxiety. Or they do not find a place in the curriculum or existing school structure. All this suggests that teachers need in-service training and support to get started with climate education.

The impact on young people

Climate change directly affects young people. The OECD conducts PISA tests on fifteen-year-old students across 37 countries, in six continents. PISA 2006 found that only one in five young people can clearly explain what is wrong with the environment.

The test also shows that young people mainly learn about environmental issues at school. Then through the media, books, the internet and a small minority through friends and family. This shows that science lessons and this knowledge go hand in hand (Coertjens et al., 2010). Young people who have less science knowledge and skills go through life with naive optimism that the problems will disappear in the future. Better understanding, however, makes young people realistic about the magnitude of climate challenges.

PISA 2018 provided new insights on the importance of young people's engagement, where they can set goals, reflect and take action. In that context, it indicated that young people themselves should have the opportunity to have a positive impact on their own lives and the world around them (Schleicher, 2019). Meanwhile, 79% of young people already know about climate change and global warming.

The usefulness of climate education

During an Open Society Foundations webinar, I ask Lorenzo Fioramonti what sound climate education consists of. Fioramonti is a former minister of education in Italy and ensured that his country was the first to include climate education in the curriculum. According to him, the key is for every age and subject to be confronted with climate. The aim is for someone graduating as a doctor or architect to be able to make sustainable decisions in their future career. He too confirms that it has a direct impact on young people's lifestyle and consumption. On average, it takes 10 to 15 years to adapt a national curriculum. Despite clear commitments to provide education on the environment at the 1992 Earth Summit, only two countries have fully integrated climate education into the curriculum so far: Italy and New Zealand. Soon Mexico will follow. There are also other ways to teach about it: as an optional lesson or as part of science or geography lessons. Italy claimed to be the first to establish a separate subject for it. In reality, this subject includes three topics - one of which is media literacy - and the teacher gets to choose from them. It is different in Portugal, where it is part of the national curriculum and the approach is project-based. In the Philippines, India, Honduras, Brazil, Ireland and other countries, the subject is discussed during science lessons. In South Africa, in turn, climate education is optional.

Small actions

Many young people confirm that the environment is important to them. As much as 78% on average. The majority of these admit to already taking small actions at home, such as turning down the heating or air conditioning. 46% are willing to make purchases ethically, even if it results in a more expensive purchase.

However, when you ask young people what they can do to tackle climate change, the percentage drops dramatically to half (57%). Even fewer fifteen-year-olds think their behaviour could have an impact on people in other countries (44%) (OECD, PISA 2018). So while many young people are aware and interested in the future of the planet, and are even starting to take responsibility in their daily lives, they do not feel they have the power to influence.

In figures

Recent research by the Brookings Institute suggests that if one in five third-grade students in high income countries were educated about climate, we would emit 19 gigatons less CO_2 by 2050. If education helps young people find solutions to climate change, it could impact their daily behaviour, reducing their carbon footprint. It also argues that if we offer education to all girls who are currently not attending school, it would lead to 85 gigatonnes less emissions by 2050. Project Drawdown provides a list of all the solutions to climate change. Providing education to girls ranks sixth in it. Preventing food waste is ranked even higher. Every year, 7 billion meals are served in schools in the US. Consequently, education has a bigger impact than installing wind turbines (47 gigatonnes) or solar power (19 gigatonnes).

In a study of 125 countries, researchers found that the deadly toll caused by floods, droughts, forest fires and extreme temperatures would be reduced by 60% if 70% more women were able to receive education by 2050. Imagine what would happen if 100% of all women could receive 12 years of education! Another importance of education is to teach young people the necessary skills so that they can better cope with the severe impacts of climate change.

Momentum

There is clearly momentum for climate education. In the US and the UK, 80% of parents are open to climate education. 86% of teachers think it should be part of the curriculum, but 60% of them feel it does not fit into their lessons. They also feel they do not have the required knowledge and resources.

Audrey Azoulay, director general of UNESCO, believes that education should empower young people to understand the current climate crisis and let them shape the future. To save our planet, we need to transform the way we live, produce, consume and interact with nature. Climate education must become fundamental, everywhere.

So education certainly has a crucial role to play, especially in terms of science subjects and a different pedagogical approach. As Thomas Friedman, columnist at *The New York Times*, puts it, 'You cannot sweet-talk Mother Nature, you cannot spin her.' Our nature always follows the principles of science and always has the last word. With every pandemic, you could argue that nature is trying to get up and recover. It is a symptom of things going wrong. What fever means to our sick bodies, COVID-19 is to a planet with a blanket that is too warm.

Change lifestyle

What is knowledge worth if children do not feel they can do something about it? In a previous chapter, we already talked about psychological factors that may or may not motivate people to do something about the climate problem in a very concrete way. In the case of children and young people, the school plays a big role. After all, the responsibility for giving pupils self-efficacy, freedom of choice, and a sense of responsibility, lies with schools. Only in this way can young people change their lifestyles, start sustainable businesses, push for innovative green technology, support ecologically sound political decisions and strike the right balance between their own needs and those of future generations. In other words, adjust their behaviour and mindset.

Education has unfortunately not been a priority as a solution to the climate crisis until today. Sound climate education can ensure that our young people make sustainable decisions - now and in the future, insights will make them change their behaviour, change the mindset of their parents, society and even world leaders.

How young people can influence their parents

Can young people positively influence their parents and change their behaviour as a result? Greta Thunberg once sat in front of the Swedish parliament on Fridays, wanting to make a strong statement for the climate. Her father indicated that she bombarded him and her mother with facts and continued to do so until he began to see the problem and found no more counter arguments. Her father became a vegetarian and her mother gave up flying, even though she is a well-known opera singer.

Indian students learn to make compost

Lawson et al. (2019) showed in a study that Thunberg is not alone. Young people may increase the degree of their parents' concern about climate change because their views - unlike those of adults - are less politically influenced. Parents are also concerned about what their children think, what occupies them and even their social engagement, also in relation to the climate. Belgian teacher Olivier Dijkmans invited parents to his classroom. In his class of 24 pupils, he counts no fewer than 16 different nationalities. By presenting their solutions to their parents, the youngsters managed to bring change at home as well. Allowing children to have a conversation with their parents (without explicitly mentioning 'climate change') has a positive chance of getting past political ideologies. The impact is greatest on energy consumption and waste production (Boudet et al., 2016).

The study shows that teaching young people about climate does cause concern among parents. This research even led to behavioural change. The greatest impact was among fathers and conservative parents. Daughters, in turn, were found to have the most impact. Lawson suspects that this can be explained by the fact that girls between the ages of 14 and 16 simply have better communication skills and more persuasion than their male peers. Nicole Holthuis of Stanford University welcomes the results. According to her, researchers too often assume that their data is enough to persuade people to change their lifestyles.

The results show that conversations between several generations can be an efficient start to fighting climate change. And through the family, society can also be influenced bottom-up, as adults can have the same conversations with friends.

Conclusion

Never were so many people worldwide educated as today, yet that world is on the brink of environmental disaster. We are capable of flying a helicopter on Mars and developing more than five pandemic vaccines within the year. What is going wrong? How can we disconnect education from an economic prosperity that often takes precedence and thwarts action for climate? Education focuses heavily on knowledge, but we should note that this is not enough to know that there is a problem.

A student shows her findings and solutions to parents in class

We need to shift the discussion from *why* governments should bring sustainable change to *how* they should do it. But there is also an individual responsibility. Through education, we must also address the causes of climate change and not just its consequences.

Inform young people in an authentic way, connect them and take it a step further by letting them find solutions too. While they have given clear signals by taking to the streets, shouting and going on strike, they have more to offer. They have the potential to take meaningful actions and modify their lifestyles and, by extension, those of friends, family and society. The potential is great and cheap at the same time. Preventing food waste at school has more potential than installing solar panels on the roof of the same school. Educating girls has more potential than building wind farms. Sometimes realisation is already a very big step. What if there was an opportunity to tackle climate change, teach future-proof skills to young people, provide crucial in-service training to teachers and improve the health of our global population with a single action? Well, that is exactly the goal of the Climate Action

Project. It is great to see that a model that works for refugee education also works for climate education.

Achieving the 1.5 degrees from the Paris Agreement and net zero by 2050 will require major behavioural change among a new generation of climate-aware and socially active citizens. Research suggests that individual behavioural changes in food, waste, agriculture and transport can reduce emissions by 20 to 37%. Education systems urgently need to give young people the knowledge, skills and mindset to act on climate in their families and communities. Climate literacy must therefore be integrated and embedded in schools and society - it must become as fundamental as learning to read and write. For this, the necessary teacher training and support is crucial. In addition, we need to focus more on vulnerable and historically marginalised groups who lose the most in the climate crisis. And give them the skills and support to thrive in a greener world.

Does education have an important role in climate education? Yes. The numbers don't lie. A common rebuttal is that it would be too slow. That we need change now. However, education offers instantaneous change. Young people change their behaviour and possibly that of family and friends, and in this way they can even influence the behaviour of society.

THE NEED FOR CLIMATE EDUCATION

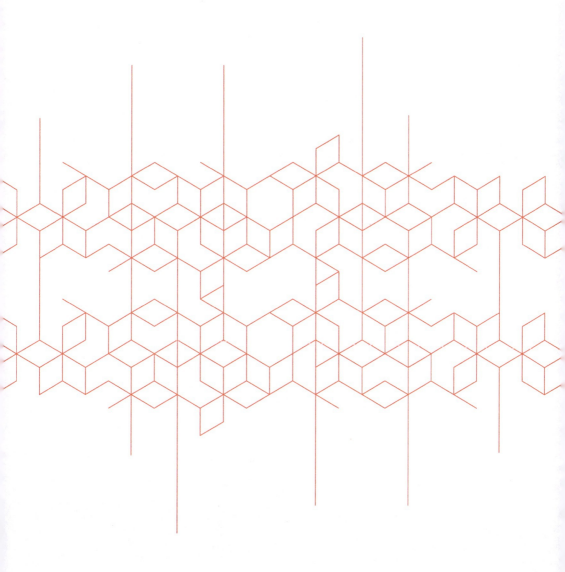

10 A BIG STEP: CLIMATE ACTION PROJECT

With 3.5 million participants, teachers and pupils across 152 countries, you could call the Climate Action Project a real movement. Anne Dolan has been able to testify first-hand about the impact of the Climate Action Project by working with Irish pupils and teachers (Dolan, 2020). Describing her experiences, she argues that children are confronted with all kinds of extracurricular messages about climate change. These can lead to confusion, and some children even become less able to understand climate change because of them. Dolan (2021) argues that climate education helps pupils to better place what they hear and experience.

Since its inception, the Climate Action Project has experienced quite a growth. Not only in size, but also in quality. At the start, I did not believe in a curriculum, because it would direct teachers too fiercely. By implication, this would give pupils less freedom to suggest topics and directions on their own. But after a few years, we did notice that some teachers even lacked knowledge about climate change or started using wrong facts. For instance, there was a teacher who told students that meteors were heading for our planet because of climate change. There was an urgent need for a curriculum that not only gives teachers the right facts, but also the pedagogical approach and required pedagogical change. In 2020, we developed this curriculum with lesson preparations in collaboration with WWF scientists. It became a challenge to ensure that teachers would not print this curriculum to hand out in full to their students. This would make instruction predominant again and leave no room for their students' input, which is crucial though.

But teachers also continued to share their clever finds. A template was created for this purpose, creating uniformity. Today, teachers have access to an extensive database of activities in various languages, for different ages and where the teacher clearly sees how long the activity takes and what materials are needed. One activity even made it to *National Geographic Junior Magazine*. Together with my son Mauro, I describe how you can make your own bioplastic with nothing but milk and vinegar, and then use a mould to design Lego men. The simple application lets students creatively see if their own concoction is sustainable and offers them deeper insights. And it's not just environmentally friendly, because imagine the sudden access to toys for children in refugee camps this way!

From idea to action

Kwauk (2020) argues that three steps are required to move from ideas to action: share expertise with teachers, learners, developers, businesses or governments; support teachers' and learners' creativity; track results to increase impact.

Mauro makes bioplastic with milk and vinegar

Six years after the launch of the Climate Action Project, the solutions that teachers developed with their students kept piling up. The creativity of both young people and teachers is limitless. I noticed that they came up with particularly inventive solutions. Inventions that silence you and make you happy.

Like the Canadian teacher Kristine Holloway, who made edible water bubbles with her 14-year-old students. These are shoots of water with an edible sleeve that looks like clear plastic. The bubbles make disposable packaging obsolete. Now what if we could ensure that everyone worldwide could make and replicate this? I asked all teachers who came up with remarkable solutions to write out their recipe or activity for colleagues and make them available as learning activities so that other teachers could replicate them.

Green Fingers

That's how US teacher Stephen Ritz described how to make vertical gardens with disposables. He made this on a large scale with his school in the Bronx to give opportunities to young people. The same Ritz also designed an activity where students have to write a letter to a plant, giving them new insights.

There are several benefits associated with plants in the classroom. Lee et al. (2005) argue that they help to take a 'brain break'. Indeed, a couple of plants in the classroom help students concentrate better and increase the ability to learn new things. Plants also provide an excellent buffer to noise (D'Alessandro et al., 2015) and refresh the air (Pegas et al., 2012). Other pupils were given responsibility for a small piece of land in their school, where their involvement and motivation increased enormously as they became responsible for the survival of plants in their own little garden. Pupils made natural fertiliser, a window farm, a water filter, handmade paper, eco-friendly soap and plantable seed paper. In Uganda, pupils set up a tree

Chinese students get a piece of land and bear responsibility for their own plants

nursery. Other groups of young people then made seed bombs that you can catapult to an inaccessible piece of land, to plant a beautiful array of plants or even trees. One group went above and beyond and sent me a video: how they used their drone to drop seed bombs in very unreachable places.

A whole range of activities

Canadian students make edible water bubbles

Young people also gained better insights. In Israel, Chicago and Spain, young people took to the streets and interviewed passersby. They took on the role of a journalist and recreated real TV studios, in which they then shot clever videos.

In New Zealand and Vietnam, youngsters went on field trips and investigated water samples. In Canada, students discovered that mealworms can digest styrofoam without getting sick. An original way to dispose of plastic waste.

In Dubai, students went to clean up beaches and elsewhere too, recycling was done in many ways. Indian youngsters, for example, found an ingenious system to develop an irrigation system via used ballpoint pens. Others made a rug from old saris (robes traditionally worn by women). In the Philippines, students made a robot out of used plastic bottles. In Croatia, a reuse point was set up. Young people could bring discarded toys and other things they no longer needed there for others to borrow.

Problems were solved in creative ways. Cooperation was crucial. In Norway, pupils applied for subsidies for solar panels for their school's roof. With success. In Albania, pupils painted the roof with lime paint to reflect the sun and cool the building.

The Climate Action Project appears to be giving students green skills that they will already need for future jobs in agriculture, manufacturing, construction, utilities, circular economy, logistics and transport. Trinomics (2022) breaks down that 26% of jobs will be impacted by the green transition started in several countries.

In Uruguay, students learnt how to create a website, giving people in their neighbourhood tips for sustainable learning. In Poland, pupils made very professional videos to demonstrate the impact of climate education and in Tunisia they developed a real game. And commitment was high. Young people in Egypt came to school every day for four weeks during the summer holidays just to be part of the project.

Students in Sierra Leone also joined despite harsh conditions

A world record was even broken in Turkey. While national television covered the action, students made the world's longest array of used batteries. They made it into the *Guinness Book of Records*.

But it was not about ingenious solutions everywhere. In some regions, it was a real chore for teachers to simply participate. Students in Sierra Leone have access to the internet only on Sundays. For teacher Miriam Mason-Sesay, sending some photos and short videos via WhatsApp is a real chore. During one video, youngsters recount how one fellow pupil died in the floods and how teacher John's house was partially destroyed. These haunting testimonies left no one cold as they were shared in classrooms across every continent. That's how you bring empathy to the classroom.

In the news

Many of these solutions, actions and stories made it to the national press. Teachers, students and school leaders received huge opportunities and appreciation as a result. In as many as 45 countries, the project was featured in newspapers, on radio and TV or in a magazine.

I distinctly remember sending some photos to *National Geographic*. I added Mike Dunlea's message, about the mother of one of the students pictured. She stressed how fiercely this project had affected her son's life. The boy had retrieved all the magazines from the attic and could now only note that he was in one edition himself. Offering opportunities and lasting memories. That is the essence of this project.

Students build experiences that they will remember in five, ten, maybe even 25 years from now.

At the end of the project, many schools organised a real graduation party, where the children received certificates. In Portugal, this even took place on a navy ship. Although this seems like a symbolic act, these certificates do have value. I learnt from the Vietnamese teacher that the document enabled her students to take up an internship abroad.

CNN reports on the Climate Action Project in Chile

Cooperation

Thanks to collaborations with LEGO and Cartoon Network, among others, we were able to take the project to the next level. Together with Cartoon Network, we set up a network of Climate Action Schools of Excellence: 250 schools worldwide that demonstrated great results and that we wanted to get to work together. They were sent a beautiful plaque to attach to the school wall.

With LEGO, we created monthly small challenges, which allowed us to keep the commitment for a whole year. These challenges required students to find a solution to a big problem each time. They then submitted these online. All solutions are good, whether they are drawings and paintings or works in cardboard or recycled plastic. We did notice that these short assignments were an enormous success. The diplomas we gave to each participant together with LEGO probably contributed to this. Vladyslav Kachur from Ukraine thanked me for these challenges, because for a while they made the students forget the sounds of the bombings.

PPP

During the project, I discovered that three factors are important and must be in balance for a project to grow remarkably: press, partners and public figures.

Partners strengthen your project. Depending on their nature, they support financially, provide credibility, or expand your reach. But partners are usually only interested when you can already put solid numbers on the table.

The press expands your reach and makes your initiatives world-famous. After each article, you can count on a lot of people responding enthusiastically and even wanting to collaborate. Some of our best collaborations with partners arose from this. The bigger the impact, the more important the media output.

Public figures can recommend your project with a quote or a video message. This gets participants very excited and also piques the interest of the press and partners. But of course, these celebrities get requests daily, and they have to be careful that their name is not linked to a shady or too small project.

In fact, when these three factors - partners, press and public figures - are balanced, a project grows exponentially. The Climate Action Project had 10.000 participants in 2017, 100.000 in 2019, 2.7 million in 2021 and 3.4 million in 2022. The remarkable growth in 2021 is due to collaboration with partners in 30 different countries that shared the project widely with teachers.

The sky is the limit

One day, I receive an email from TJ. Thomas Anthony Jones is an American actor and producer who stars in *Grey's Anatomy* and *NCIS*. Together with Jasmine Hester (*9-1-1* and *The Last Ship*), he requests an online meeting. When I first speak to them, I see two amazing people asking to be involved in the project. They will travel to countries to record videos and deliver solutions developed by students to local people. They recently took a flight to Kenya with solar lamps on board. Thanks to them, 200 families in the slums of Kibera have free light at night so that young people can study. And during the day … the lights recharge. This completes the circle. Findings by Portuguese and Canadian students who took part in the project are now brought to people in need. Their video stories will in turn inspire new young people to come up with new clever solutions.

The power of cultural diversity

In 2019, I teach climate and sustainability to Chinese students in Beijing for one week. During a presentation attended by a hundred and fifty youngsters, I mention Greta Thunberg and spontaneous boos sound in the auditorium. All the teachers present are startled. Do these students have doubts about climate change? Are they tired of being confronted with it? After speaking to some attendees individually, nothing could be further from the truth. They do not agree with Greta, and they do not like the fact that she is heavily on the verbal attack against world leaders. In Chinese culture, you don't lash out at elders; there is respect for parents and world leaders. Almost we had drawn the wrong conclusions, but this example gave us a nice insight into how diverse cultures can be. I also dream away and think back to the Human Differences project, where I noticed that cultural diversity is not always easy to cope with for teachers and pupils.

The physician and professor Hans Rosling, who died in 2017, was an inspired speaker whose data provide insights into misconceptions about inequalities between developing and developed countries. His application *Dollar Street*, part of the website Gapminder, shows very visually what inequalities are like in many countries. Through photos, he shows how toys, teeth and toilets, among other things, look different in Norway, Burkina Faso or Haiti.

Culturally responsive teaching (CRT) (Ladson-Billings, 1995) is a method that focuses on differences in culture, language and life experiences. CRT can be applied in a classroom where there are children from diverse backgrounds. But CRT can equally well be applied in global exchanges during a project. The approach is very close to self-discovery learning and PBL. According to Hammond (2014), every student has different talents and strengths, tinged by their cultural background, which should be utilised during the lesson. It offers the advantage of reaching all students in the class and raising expectations. In addition, it strengthens competences such as empathy, where students understand cultural differences better. Ultimately, it can make pupils more appreciative of each other.

There is a tremendous strength in global projects because it creates an interesting mix of different cultures, languages, backgrounds, religions and customs. Because everyone shares the same mission, it creates a deep connection. People learn to appreciate each other, learn from each other's differences and feel like they have friends in other parts of the world, even though they have often never met and never will. Remarkably, this cultural factor is almost always overlooked in research publications on education. The researcher is conducting a test in a limited group, which is mostly located in one particular place. So, to understand the power of education and estimate the scope of the global factor, you always have to factor in cultural diversity.

Conclusion

It was during a stay in Bangalore, India that I learnt about the United Nations' (seventeen) Sustainable Development Goals (SDGs), which were released in 2015 and are promoted as global Sustainable Development Goals. It was the start of a new initiative, 'Where have all the sparrows gone?', after discovering that in some places (London, many Indian cities, and so on) the sparrow is disappearing. The idea of the project was that students would try to find out what caused this disappearance and figure out potential solutions. The initiative had a small scope, but helped me gain more insights into the educational value of the SDGs, one of which is climate action.

My friend Michael Soskil once said: 'It's hard to change the world if you know little about it.' Besides learning about climate change, finding possible options and taking positive actions, virtual interactions remain a crucial part of the project. Students get to know people in other countries and even continents. It is an example of technology transforming the classroom. But this exchange also often leads to powerful collaborations and appreciation.

Expert learning would also become an important part of the project. And that grew into a major event.

A BIG STEP: CLIMATE ACTION PROJECT

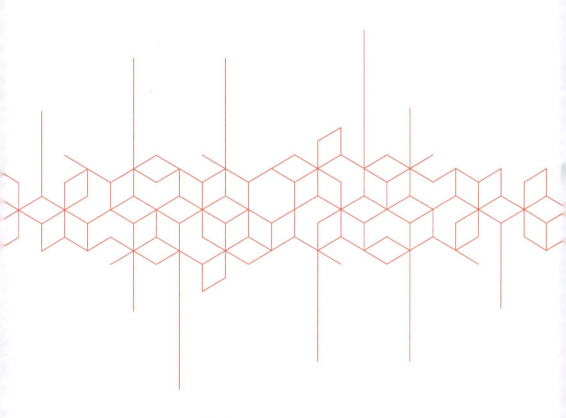

11 CLIMATE ACTION DAY

'You're the wrong Koen', Jane Goodall said to me when I knocked on her hotel room door. I was perplexed for a moment and my decision not to prepare a consultation with her suddenly turned out to be a very bad idea. To keep the conversation spontaneous, unprepared seemed like a better option. After all, we had just built two schools together. One in Gombe, where she started her world-renowned research on chimpanzees 60 years ago. The other in Pugu, in the other windward direction of Tanzania, where Jane stays twice a year.

Jane welcomes me to her hotel room. She is in Belgium for two days and this evening I speak at her gala. But first a personal meeting, for which I am feeling very nervous. To make matters worse, she waits for my initiative to start the conversation. Tanya, the head of Jane Goodall Institute Belgium, tells Jane that I look nervous and this turns the mood around. Jane tells a funny anecdote and a naughty joke. As she explains it with a lot of laughter, tears roll down her cheeks and she guffaws. It will forever be our joke, known only to a handful of insiders. The night ends with some people from her organisation all drinking a glass of whisky in her hotel room. A tradition. Relaxed, I look back on a fruitful day and contemplate the interactions between Jane and people who care deeply about nature.

It was Shweta from India who saw videos of our school in Kakuma in 2018. And it seemed like a good idea to her to build schools in Tanzania too. Talking about her plans, she mentioned Roots & Shoots, an initiative unknown to me at the time. Only when I had confirmed to build a first school did I learn that this was Jane Goodall's youth initiative. I have always looked up to Jane and other people who made a big difference with a discovery, action or vision. In 2018, I also wanted nothing more than to build as many schools as possible for the weak. On a map, I pinned Palestine, Argentina, Morocco, and other places. But it soon dawned on me that it is enormously difficult to find parties willing to pay for all this infrastructure. That school in Tanzania did materialise, and in the middle of the jungle. We launched the school in style: in the presence of Jane, who had a team from *National Geographic* in her wake. She made an inspired speech to the youngsters and I listened in via videoconference. She was disappointed that I had not travelled down to Tanzania myself. Fifteen minutes of her documentary 'Jane, the Hope' is dedicated to our school. That was my first introduction to Jane, who I would subsequently interview twice more online in front of an audience of half a million people. When she visited Belgium once more in 2022, I was happy to see her again. This time with my son Mauro, who told me that meeting Jane would mean a lot to him. The fact that he doesn't speak English and was only eleven years old didn't seem to be a problem.

Unlike last time, the conversation starts with a hearty hug. We discuss the importance of climate education and look back over the past few years. Jane intersperses everything with funny events that have happened to her and urges me to translate some pieces for Mauro. She asks him what he wants to do when he grows up and writes a personal message for him in a book. Again, she has inspired one person who will in turn do the same to others.

In 2018, I was nominated for the Global Teacher Prize, an initiative of the Varkey Foundation and considered worldwide as the Nobel Prize for Education. In an elimination race, the fifty, ten and then the best teacher in the world are announced. These revelations are not simply made via e-mail. They are done in style and with bravado. For instance, it was Bill Gates who announced that I was one the ten best teachers in the world. A month later, we are called on stage one by one by Trevor Noah, the famous host of *The Daily Show*. The stakes are high and nerves are extremely tense: the winner gets a million dollars and knows his life will change dramatically. A day earlier, the media tipped me as the winner. The fact that I got to invite three journalists from newspapers and TV channels was also strange. They followed me in Dubai for a whole week, where I spoke at the 'Global Education & Skills Forum' event and gave interviews to journalists from 20 different countries. I get a call from the BBC and have to turn down an interview. Too busy, let's do it in two hours. I proofread a newspaper article for publication and look up. There are three rows of people in front of me. Some want to give me a small gift from their country. Others want to ask something. To possibly make things even busier, my friends Michael, Armand, Elisa, Jelmer and I have decided to launch our book. We spent the past year writing the book *Teaching in the Fourth Industrial Revolution* and sit together at regular intervals to sign books. I give one to the education ministers of Palestine and Argentina. Then again, the advantage is that this is not an event where I have to walk off the kilos afterwards ...

Just before the announcement, we go to the green room. This is a room where celebrities meet and talk. I see one of the other candidates for the prize still nervously scribbling together a speech. He is visibly confused. Others have their interpreters with them because they don't speak English. We drop in to take a photo with Trevor Noah and Charlize Theron. They clearly have the highest status in this room. Meanwhile, three cool guys approach me. One of them gives me a handshake like I've never received one before. I give a shout and his colleague gives him a reprimand. He tells me he is preparing for a role for a film in which he will play Elton John. I wonder aloud if he is that strong. The three gentlemen laugh. They suggest taking a selfie. Later, I discover that these cool dudes were world-renowned actors Taron Egerton and Nicholas Hoult. I still don't know the name of the third one, although I recognise him from several films. A little later, I greet a handsome Indian lady. She is silent but her look tells me that she too is here for a reason. A few days later, I discover that I was photographed with Priyanka Chopra, one of India's best-known actresses, who has hundreds of millions of followers on social media. But, more importantly, she is also a role model for charities. My turn to have my picture taken with Charlize and Trevor. A fellow contestant wants to take a picture with my phone but does so in portrait mode. This is a my hobby horse. I think that photos should always be taken in landscape mode because that way no arms and other essential body parts are cut. Charlize laughs and says that she learnt something today. It only makes the photo more captivating. Unlike others, I don't care about the photo. In seven seconds, I want to tell Charlize what my goal is in the Kenyan refugee camp AND get her contact details so I can ask her to support the project. It works. It will be the first quote from a global star endorsing the Kakuma project. Later, it will be a game changer that will set off a string of other recommendations from the Dalai Lama, Queen Elizabeth II, Jennifer Morgan, head of Greenpeace, and Helen Clark, the popular former prime minister of New Zealand.

It is time to enter the beautiful hall of the famous Atlantic Hotel. The location could be worse. We are in the most expensive hotel on the Palm, the artificial islands. Guests are served cappuccinos and desserts adorned with gold leaf. Sitting in the front row are all the world leaders and celebrities I have met before. Al Gore, former Britain's prime minister Tony Blair and Nicolas Sarkozy, the president of France, greet each other. Charlize takes a picture of us which she will later post on Instagram. Lewis Hamilton arrives in a Lamborghini and brings the gold trophy. I look at my wife in the audience and realise that Mauro and my parents are watching via the internet. Colleagues even gather on Sunday to hear the results live at school.

Trevor Noah, Koen Timmers and Charlize Theron

Global Teacher Prize

The announcement is chaotic. The organisers had the original idea of sharing a video message in which hundreds of children announce the winner's name together. But ... no one understands the winner's name. It is the brilliant Andria Zafirakou who wins the grand prize. She has an exceptional year ahead in which she will be awarded a noble title in England and a street name in Cyprus.

The first feeling I have is disappointment of course. The competition beast in me is cast down. And my first task is to speak to the press and go to the after-party. There I see a mob of women walking behind Lewis Hamilton, begging for a photo. Lewis sees me and gives me an even firmer handshake. What a primal power this man has. He suggests taking a selfie, creating jealousy among the group of women. A firm handshake apparently does not mean a steady hand. The photo turns out to be blurred. I pass the mob and receive a lot of angry looks. The second photo does turn out to be successful. A nice trophy that I pull out every year when Lewis becomes Formula 1 world champion yet again.

This Global Teacher Prize has changed the walk of life of many a teacher. Two of them became ministers of education. Some travelled the world to give talks, or wrote a book. Others broke down completely. For me, above all, it has created a huge forum to promote my projects.

The Climate Action Project was often about giving opportunities to young people. Interacting with interesting people, experts and even celebrities is something that became more and more relevant after a while. Often it were teachers participating in the project who came up with interesting speakers. For instance, I met Matt Larsen-Daw from WWF Great Britain, who was happy to share his inspiring story with participants during a webinar. Via Twitter, I spoke to Rick Davis, who calls himself 'redplanetrick'. It was Rick who congratulated me on the project. Only later did I discover that he is the person at NASA responsible for the landing site of a future Mars mission. He was involved in several space missions to the International Space Station (ISS) and in steering the Perseverance Rover. When I did a first webinar with him and his assistant Bob, I couldn't help but think for a moment that these two gentlemen must be at least ten times smarter than me. I sat in my seat like petrified. But over the years, a friendship grew, and the short meetings would become moments to look forward to. And out of those moments opportunities invariably arose. Similarly, Rick and Bob would address the participants. Their main intention was to inspire students and make them realise that no matter what country they lived in, what gender or origin, anyone could become the first astronaut to travel to Mars. But during our meetings we also launched crazy ideas: shall we have students send a message to ISS astronauts? And so it happened in 2021. Students were allowed to send in a message of hope of up to two hundred characters via the Climate Action Project website. These were all put on a chip and sent to ISS. Our Message to Space was yet another initiative to give students around the world a fond memory.

But as time went on, we got more and more interesting connections and wondered: what if we launched one big online event? Climate Action Day was a reality. We launched it on 5 November 2020 and the intention was that the event would also be the project's closing event. What we saw at the time was that the show often revolved around the speakers or presenters. We wanted to do that differently. Jennifer Williams and I would host the event; the students, their solutions and their questions would be the basis for the event. We also wanted inspiring experts, ministers, celebrities, representatives of major organisations and presidents to share their message and answer students' questions in less than 15 minutes.

During Jane Goodall's event, I had the pleasure of sitting next to Princess Esmeralda of Belgium. I got that honour because I spoke at the gala. Esmeralda is the sister of the former and aunt of the current king. Looking at the beautifully set table, I could already tell from the name cards that I would be surrounded by many people of nobility. I did not expect some of them to be displeased sometime later that it would be me and not them sitting next to the princess. I just managed to prevent my name tag from being moved and heard someone ask, 'C'est qui ce Timmèrs?' As the evening progressed, I got to know the princess as a journalist and activist. We maintained contact. During a climate march in New York, she sent me a message and so we ended up in a large crowd of people listening to Greta Thunberg. Esmeralda introduced me to Kumi Naidoo, a South African activist who previously headed Greenpeace and Amnesty International. We rounded off our day with a coffee at Starbucks in the heart of New York. Two people on the same mission, from very different backgrounds, who became friends.

Both Esmeralda and Kumi would speak at our first Climate Action Day. Kumi even created a poem especially for it. Esmeralda suggested Vanessa Nakate to speak and asked her questions like an accomplished journalist. Vanessa is an Ugandan climate activist who became known in a way no one wishes. She was invited with Greta Thunberg and three more activists to speak at the World Economic Forum in

Davos. She arrived with only a small backpack full of T-shirts in a snowy city where world leaders and the press flocked. And there a famous photo was taken of five young activists, of whom Vanessa was the only African one. Press agency AP had no better idea than to cut her, as the only black person, from the photo. The image thus went around the world, to the horror of Nakate who argued that an entire continent was erased from this important conversation.

Jane Goodall also agreed to an interview. Arranging an interview with the famous television producer David Attenborough proved much more difficult. But thanks to our connection with Matt, it still became a reality. He made a video message for young people. Esmeralda also put us in touch with young activist Helena Gualinga from Ecuador and Sandrine Dixson-Declève, who heads the influential Club of Rome. She was a major force behind the Paris climate agreement. Setting up such an event proved to be a feat. We ended up with an online and live show of no less than eight hours that we streamed for free on YouTube and social media. Even during the show, the Portuguese education minister confirmed his attendance. Ministers from the UK, South Africa and Ethiopia also addressed our audience. We had a Nobel Prize winner, members of the European Parliament and the European Commission, the president of Macedonia and delegates from the United Nations. We came up with the idea of going a step further to enforce certain promises. For instance, Yvonne Aki-Sawyerr, the mayor of Freetown, the capital of Sierra Leone, promised to plant a large number of trees. And Ronilda Co from the Philippine Department of Education promised to partner with us to work on climate education. One of my personal highlights was an interview with former Colombian president Juan Manuel Santos, whom I met earlier in Dubai. Our first Climate Action Day reached 20.000 teachers and, through them, 200.000 students.

Since our climate project focuses very much on action and because we believe in collaborative education, we did not want to create an event where young people have to listen for hours. For the next editions, we wanted to activate and innovate our students more. I explored the idea of involving absolute world stars, but had to find out that a video message of a no more than five minutes costs 200.000 euros. Princess Esmeralda was at it again, bringing activists Kaossara Sani from Togo and Martina Fjällberg from Sweden. Diversity and spread across all continents are crucial for us. These editions could count on the message of Presidents James Alix Michel of Seychelles and Tarja Halonen of Finland, as well as several ministers from Morocco, Costa Rica, Jamaica and Moldova. Our friends at NASA arranged for students to ask questions to astronaut TJ Creamer. This was a fantastic moment because the students we asked to ask a question had a disability. Their first question was fantastic: 'Have you ever seen an alien?'

In Antarctica, there are only two schools. The teacher of one of these schools addresses the audience in a video message and explains how they have been able to participate, despite the extreme weather conditions they have to deal with. Juan Pablo Celis Garcia of UN Environment Programme argues that we need young innovators who can find solutions. The 2020 event is streamed live at WWF's booth at COP 26 in Glasgow.

It has always been my wish to have the Pope speak at an event. However, it is proving very difficult to get near him. You can only speak to the Vatican if someone introduces you there. After much writing back and forth, it turned out that the pope was too weakened, and Cardinal Peter Turkson would do the honours. When you launch a live event, you have two big fears: speakers who don't show up or speakers who don't keep to the set time. In both scenarios, the whole schedule falls apart.

Amercan Students students watch an interview with Jane Goodall during Climate Action Day

But Cardinal Turkson, who prepared more than fifty slides and obviously would not keep to his ten minutes of speaking time, could definitely count on our sympathy when he was called repeatedly during his presentation. We alternated those moments with a magician doing some tricks with the youngsters online. We also tried to amaze young people. For instance, a Cartoon Network character spoke to the audience and the voice actor behind the character showed how the filming is done. We snared adventurer James Levelle, OECD's Andreas Schleicher, Kenyan activist Elizabeth Wathuti, filmmaker Ellen Windemuth and young drummer and influencer Nandi Bushell. Youth author Georgina Stevens handed out no less than five hundred e-books. And then suddenly we got a miraculous message. We would have a speaker everyone knows. Someone who was passionate about climate action and would want to address our audience briefly. It were our friends from The World's Largest Lesson who convinced Prince William to do it.

The event also empowered our project as many speakers agreed to serve on our advisory panel. Climate Action Day takes place annually in November and information about this can be accessed on climateactionday.net.

Our main motivation is to create memories. Climate Action Day is one way of making the impact of our project visible. Not only experts and celebrities are given a forum to speak, but students also get the chance to show their work. There are also other ways to visualise the impact though.

Climate Action Day 2022

12 IMPACT

When I talk to others about the project, they react in various ways. But everyone is positive. Teachers mainly focus on the fact that their pupils are engaged and that they themselves are happy to be part of a global network. Some even report that the project has a positive impact on their pupils' grades. Then there are the media, which are mainly interested in gripping stories and anecdotes. Because those fuel the story. In turn, well-known people are impressed by the size of our network. It was Stephen Ritz who made me realise that I should not respond to every request to speak at events, podcasts or interviews. While it is true that you usually help build their story, it contributes little to the growth of your own project indeed. I began to notice that there are various groups, all with their own interests: teachers, media, funders, celebrities and scientists. And all these groups in different positions also want to see different results to judge the impact of climate education.

Among scientists, I noticed only lukewarm enthusiasm when I talked about our work. I realised that pedagogy and anecdotes are not that relevant to them. They speak the language of climate. And that's why I began to wonder how we could demonstrate the impact of climate education to them too. After all, the pedagogical approach can be measured by what the students have learnt. The marketeer and the funder look mainly at the number of participants and their geographical presence. But what is a climate scientist interested in? In CO_2. After all, that is the essence of climate change: emissions. So I wondered how to link learning materials to CO_2. There are already a lot of apps that calculate people's carbon footprints. But those apps visualise their current lifestyle. And so I thought it would be better to develop an app that students, teachers, parents and other adults can use to adjust their existing behaviour while seeing the impact. For instance, young people could go to school by bike instead of by car, eat less red meat once a week, use their smartphone less or take a shower instead of a bath. I got the idea when I first saw young activists being interviewed by TV. They may have had a lot of passion and concern, but their arguments showed that they had little background on climate change. But if these young people are already clueless about what they can do themselves, what about others? I learnt that many people do not know that eating red meat - especially lamb - has a heavy impact on the environment, or that LED

Peruvian students celebrate cycling and ask their parents to change transport

Spanish students use the app to record their personal actions

bulbs are much more economical than traditional incandescent bulbs. But if for every action you show the impact with the amounts of CO avoided$_2$, you do have something powerful. And so the desire grew to develop an app that shows young people the impact of their actions, while also providing insight into behavioural change. The icing on the cake is that the app could be used during the climate project, to show the impact by means of CO_2.

There are actions that directly affect the amount of greenhouse gases emitted, for example when people stop their polluting behaviour and behave more sustainably (Stern, 2000). This includes turning down their thermostat, generating solar energy and travelling by public transport instead of by car. There are also actions that can have an indirect influence on reducing greenhouse gas emissions, for example by influencing climate policies or accepting climate policies (Stern, 2000). Both actions should appear in the app. For the actions with indirect influence, the user could send an e-mail to the press or government, but also, for example, to a teacher asking him to participate in the Climate Action Project. For the actions with direct influence, we needed a powerful algorithm that calculates CO_2 emissions for each action. Deloitte Foundation was generous enough to bring in its design & sustainability team to develop a beautiful app with correct algorithm. New features were also added to each version: the ability to work together in teams, challenges where classes compete against each other, gamification where the user is rewarded with levels and badges. But also an extended application where you can plant a tree and pin it on a world map. This allows me to keep track of how many trees and what species are planted per country. And see pictures of that. We decided to focus not only on climate, but also on the plastic issue. To address this, the app offers tips and opportunities to avoid single use plastic and record relevant actions.

The app was enthusiastically received and won an award at the SETT fair in Belgium. Together with Hogeschool PXL, ten thousand students did a challenge across departments to find out who took the most action for the climate. We launched the app in 2020 during the Climate Action Project; we continue to add new features every month. The app was downloaded more than eight thousand times. The month after the launch, we avoided as much as 3,000 tonnes of CO_2. A great start, when you know that one adult consumes 5 to 10 tonnes of CO_2 per year, depending on the country he lives in. This figure would have to be reduced to 2.5 tonnes worldwide to achieve the climate goals.

Thanks to the app, we were able to go a step further. For example, we found out that the cost of avoiding 1 tonne of CO_2 through climate education is 0.29 euros. Remarkably cheaper than other alternatives such as tree planting (152 euros) and wind energy (50 euros) (Gillingham and Stock, 2018).

Yet we have not yet realised the full potential of the app. Only a small percentage of Climate Action Project participants use the app. Even though teachers can record the effort of students under thirteen, we find that we still need to promote the app more.

The impact of the project should not be expressed only in terms of CO_2. Policymakers told us that the solution lies mainly in innovation and technology. After all, it is a combination of individual action, tree planting, laws and education that will have to provide a solution to climate change. What was missing for me in this explanation is that we need to make students aware. If they do not know what their government stands for, their vote may unknowingly choose governments that will not commit to climate goals. In addition, not all impacts are immediate. During further studies, young people may choose to start a PhD on climate-related issues or consciously look for green jobs. Not every impact can be captured in figures.

You can find the app on earthproject.org.

IMPACT

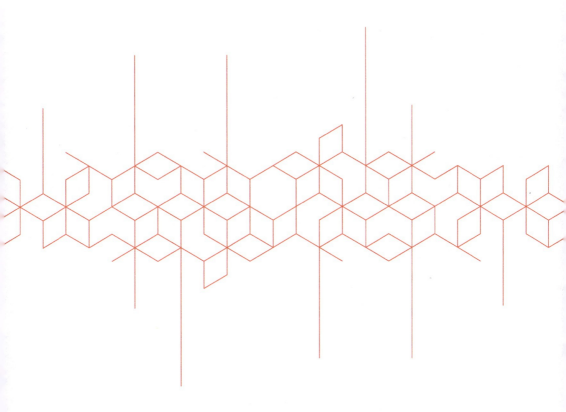

13 SOLVING WORLD PROBLEMS THROUGH EDUCATION

In 1894, there was a major crisis. Scientists predicted that in the 20th century there would be a huge problem with ... horse manure. Indeed, the horse was the most important means of transport, and by 1900, three million New Yorkers depended on it for their daily existence. More specifically, this meant that a hundred thousand horses provided 1.2 million kilograms of horse dung every day. Scientists predicted that if the population continued to rise at this rate, the streets of major cities would be buried under metres of horse manure. In 1903, the first Ford was sold. Sometimes science can get it badly wrong by not taking into account a new innovation.

Building blocks

How do you solve world problems through education? Climate change, poverty, gender inequality, violence and so on are not small problems. Yet it is important to realise that you can change someone's behaviour and mindset through education. In both Project Kakuma and the Climate Action Project, it became clear that young people's mindsets changed through interactions they had. It is now time to unveil a framework of building blocks that I identified during all the projects. These building blocks can all be deployed in the classroom. The higher you go to the top, the more impact and engagement, but also the more complicated it gets to achieve the process. It is up to the teacher to decide how far they want to go.

1   Knowledge

Pupils should have the necessary prior knowledge on a given topic. The most efficient way to provide this knowledge is through direct instruction. Certain topics are challenging and for these topics the prior knowledge is often lacking. What is a refugee, what is the greenhouse effect, net zero or adaptation? The teacher explains these terms and makes sure the students are entirely ready for the next phase.

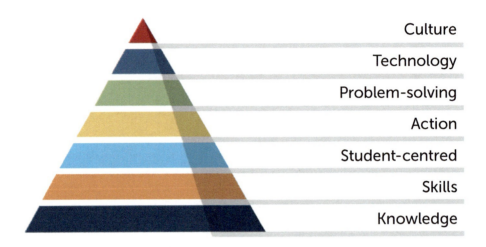

2 Skills

Students should be given the opportunity to be creative, collaborative and think critically in the process. As a teacher, try to bring a good dose of empathy into the classroom. Let pupils present their work and communicate clearly. These are the skills that are crucial in our future jobs - which is why they are often called 21st-century skills. Skills that often come with the necessary commitment from students.

3 Student-centred

I try to let my son make his own choices and do not impose sustainability or other values. However, I notice that he and his 11-year-old friends are very concerned about climate. Once I heard his group of friends brainstorming about the future of the sustainable car. They are naturally concerned about our planet. It would be extremely unfortunate if this passion is broken down by formal education.

To maintain pupils' interests and passions, but also to put pupils at the centre of their own learning, you can give them the chance to show in which direction they want to go and which problems they want to solve exactly. From now on, the teacher becomes a mentor and guide, making sure that pupils use the right resources and keep working in the right direction. He can prepare for this by acquiring the right context. For instance, it is crucial that students do not start working with wrong facts and data. Teaching the same lesson in two or more different groups is likely to lead to outliers.

4 Action

In education, we must dare to go beyond just learning about something. Through small, positive actions, we can make a big difference. Planting a tree, setting up a school garden, visiting and supporting the community ... The result is not only in this action, but also in the impact the action has on the student. For some, these are moments they carry with them for a long time and inspire them to do more.

5 Problem-solving

By finding solutions to world problems, you allow pupils to make a real difference. STEM (Science, Technology, Engineering, Math) can be used to craft real solutions. A solution can also be a drawing, prototype or concept and does not have to consist of expensive materials - it does not even have to work. On the internet, you can also find lots of solutions that you can replicate. So you are not obliged to come up with new solutions.

6 Technology

Through technology, you can transform a classroom. Through simple tools, you can make connections with other classes, even in other countries. You can bring an expert into your classroom or share your findings with others in other ways. You can visualise information more clearly, let students collaborate efficiently or differentiate better.

7 Culture

Thanks to technology, you bring the world into your classroom. By speaking to students from other cultures, languages and customs, you broaden perspectives and an appreciation grows. You can even find solutions to each other's problems, making a substantial difference.

When all these building blocks are woven into a project, pupils come close to changing behaviour, as all aspects of the world problem are touched, pupils' engagement is sensitively increased and learning becomes more authentic.

When I was eighteen, my teacher, Philippe, told me that as a human being you should try to be a seer. He was a neat man, and you could see that he had a lot going for him. He spoke as many as fifteen languages and once we were able to get him to showcase that. He was a teacher who commanded respect with his skills. In life, you have to try to see added values and details, he said. In doing so, dare to dive below the surface.

My student, Roger, once told me that he never went to sleep if there was something he did not yet know the answer to. If this were the case, he looked it up in the encyclopaedia first. That way, he became a sponge absorbing knowledge.

Let us have the same impact on our students and also make them global citizens with an eye for detail, who are driven and ever curious.

Now that the framework has been unveiled, I would like to provide another roadmap for concrete planning and implementation of projects through PBL.

The PBL roadmap to tackle world problems

Project-based learning (PBL) exposes gaps in student learning. Based on a study by Kelleher and Whitman (2018) and what I learnt from the global projects I launched, I offer steps that specifically help you plan, design and implement a project through which you want to address specific world issues in your lessons.

STEP 1 Make sure you are well prepared

Feel whether the pupils are open to a project and question them via a feedback form. Before starting the project, make sure everyone has the required prior knowledge. Does everyone know what is required to succeed? If not, teach about it. Make your students think about their prior knowledge first. Then build basic knowledge and skills. You keep doing this so that this knowledge enters long-term memory and students have prior knowledge of the subject.

STEP 2 Set up projects with a good cause

There are many world problems. Solving problems means understanding people and empathising with them. Look for problems that can be solved in your local community and find ways for your students to talk to these communities about how these problems affect them. Realise that not all the problems you are trying to solve are world-class. A clear understanding of the purpose and relevance of the project increases pupils' motivation and pushes them to dig deeper, in order to complete a challenging project.

Add choice elements and let students have a say. Kidd et al. (2012) argue that the problem to be solved should neither be too easy nor too difficult. But also that too much choice can impede learning, just as a shop shelf with too many similar items leads to decision stress and therefore can hinder a purchase.

STEP 3 Make projects highly collaborative and socially engaging

Prepare your students to use technology required for collaboration. Make sure your learners are productive and take enough time to explain to them how the tools they will need to use work. If you are working on a global level, take into account local conditions such as language, political sensitivities and time zones.

Projects require a lot of independent work and demand a lot of executive ability. Set clear goals and support planning, choosing strategies, self-monitoring, making adjustments and deciding when to finish.

Let young people simply be themselves sometimes and enjoy each other's presence. Do not underestimate the importance of their mutual social interactions. Try to dismantle the obstinate, problematic phenomenon of 'one pupil does all the work'. It is very important that group members have roles and help each other, and that their contributions are tested discreetly so that responsibilities become clear. Change roles and responsibilities during the course of the project so that learners do not start limiting themselves. As a teacher, make sure you supervise this process well and that pupils start working with correct facts and information. When you notice that they do not understand certain concepts, switch back to direct instruction.

STEP 4 Keep equality and accessibility at the forefront at all times

Make sure the student are not only working on the project after school hours. Personally, I am a strong advocate of having the entire project done in class. Prevent parents from doing the work and make sure there is no inequality between young people in terms of the amount of materials available to them at home. Provide real-time feedback. Clear, supportive and specific feedback during the learning itself is hugely valuable (Van den Branden, 2015). Learners should be given the opportunity to act according to the feedback.

STEP 5 Share experiences and celebrate impact

When students have gained new insights, it is time to share them with each other. This can be done in class, but also within the school, between schools or even globally. Stick findings, and solutions on walls and use digital alternatives so that students are proudly confronted with their work. In the final phase, make sure there is a good synthesis and that all parts are well summarised. Discuss what a possible extension might be.

Celebrate the impact if possible and be creative.

STEP 6 Make projects transformative

One of the clever things that social media enable is the creation of groups where students and graduates meet and learn from each other. Try to encourage them to continue even long after the students involved have graduated. Good projects can mark a year and transform a life. They ensure that attitudes, character and knowledge are developed.

SOLVING WORLD PROBLEMS THROUGH EDUCATION

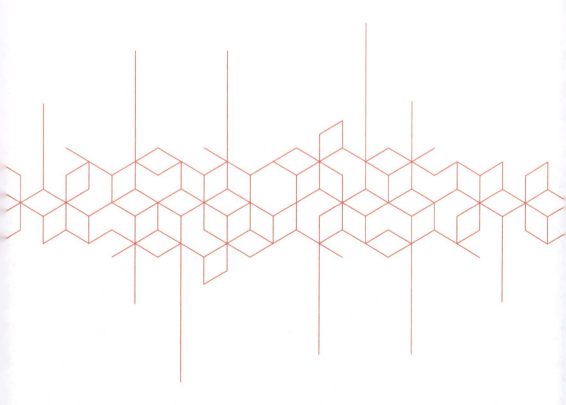

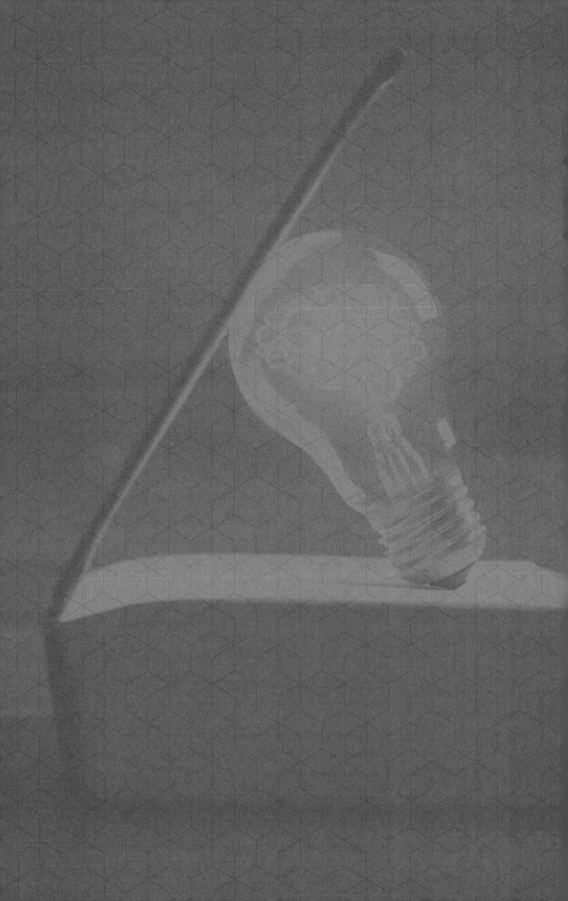

14 FROM TEACHER TO NGO

With a world-class project, you need a solid organisation and a team working together to take the project to higher levels. Only ... I never intended to run a large NGO. But a project with millions of participants requires a whole team to provide support, maintain platforms, keep curricula and lesson preparations up-to-date, answer questions, create the programme of the next Climate Action Day and so many other tasks. A team needs volunteers, but inevitably you need some professionals to take on special tasks: web developers, content development, design and marketing ... And because the team needs to be paid: accounting and fundraising. And when you talk about a team, a charity and funding, you have to look for a legal structure to set up the non-profit organization. It was exactly that search for funds that would cause many sleepless nights ...

One day, Jennifer notified me that she was going to give a presentation in Brussels. Dr Jennifer Williams was a professor at Saint Leo University in Florida and founded the 'Teach SDGs' network, to bring together all like-minded teachers who wanted to bring the SDGs into the classroom. Jennifer and I had worked together before, after we got to know each other on Twitter. A platform that was close to both of our hearts. Knowing that Jennifer would only have ten minutes between her presentations and that Brussels was a one-and-a-half-hour drive - by Belgian standards, quite a trip - it was a rather impulsive moment. A few hours later, we brainstormed about a collaboration. A few weeks later, a new NGO saw the light of day: Take Action Global, or TAG. TAG would bring together and professionalise all our global educational initiatives. And TAG would have two directors who would later prove to be very complementary.

When I founded the Climate Action Project and the Kakuma Project, the starting point was a mission. Perhaps it was even an experiment with good intentions. But the stunning results and the enthusiastic teachers involved in the projects made it impossible to stop the growth. The projects gave enormous energy. But the reality was that I used the salary I earned over the years as a teacher to fund the projects. Now that TAG would take over these projects, there were two concerns: where would we find the necessary funds and how would all the teachers involved react?

Because a project launched by a volunteer or by an organisation is perceived differently by the teachers involved. For instance, I noticed that initially there might have been some uncertainty among some participants from the first hour indeed. Moreover, small mistakes by volunteers are condoned, but less so those of organisations.

There is one thing TAG has done completely differently from other NGOs. Practically every organisation starts with an idea, builds a Theory of Change and a business plan around it. Only when they have been able to raise the necessary funds do they start their work. Some organisations are given budgets and only then even start looking into how to use this money. TAG already owned a project with hundreds of thousands of participants, already had the support of world leaders, was already covered by media from 40 countries and was already having a lot of impact. Naively, we argued that fundraising would therefore be easy. I soon discovered that local businesses and organisations had no interest in supporting a world-class project. It was simply ... too big. If we wanted to bring climate education to a particular city, the local bakery would have been interested. But global players also found it difficult. We discovered that funds can be of various origins: philanthropists, companies, grants and governments. And each type of organisation also needs a different approach and pitch. A social entrepreneur who now works at Facebook once told me that only one in 60 applications is successful. That is not an encouraging figure. Several people told me that you only receive money when your mindset is ready for it. I can tell you that this kind of science does not help you when you can barely keep your head above water. What did become clear is that everyone has their own opinions and was very helpful with advice. People are not likely to give you a donation, but they do like to see you succeed.

I am on a flight to Ibiza. Never before have I been on a plane with so many people drunk. When I arrive at my destination, abundant sunshine and blue skies are lacking. The first stop is at a shop to buy a coat. The first five taxi drivers refuse to take me to where I am going to speak. 'This address does not exist,' they state. I am on my way to an event organised by ThreeFold, which is run by Kristof de Spiegeleer. Having founded - and then sold - a whole series of successful companies, he is on a grand mission. More specifically, he wants his organisation to develop a decentralised and fair internet. An internet that guarantees privacy and security and where you can communicate and find information without ads. To this end, he is developing his own tool for video conferencing, a wiki, an office and even a crypto currency. And so I end up in a breathtaking villa overlooking the sea, where I present TAG's project. A villa with organic coffee, nice, affluent people and a cinema room where I start my presentation. After the presentation, I look up and see that people in the audience are very moved by my words. After the applause, a few come to me with tears rolling down their cheeks. I certainly hadn't felt this coming … I realise that all the clever things that happen become lists of facts in my head. But which do still inspire and even move people. Kristof looks at his wife Isabelle and together they express their desire to sponsor a nice amount of money so that TAG has a good start.

It is thanks to these successes that you gain confidence to ask for new funds. In that respect, it is somewhere true that your attitude towards money is decisive. Yet Jennifer and I do things differently. We prioritise our team and combine our job as teachers with TAG for years to come. A difficult path, but the right one for us.

We also noticed a lot of despair in the eyes of the people we asked for support. An organisation that offers education to refugees and works on climate education has its complications. To be able to shift to a higher level, we decided to hand over Project Kakuma to a Belgian non-profit organisation and to focus fully on climate education with TAG.

After ThreeFold, other organisations followed in support. In our search for funding, we tried to stay away from greenwashing. With greenwashing, companies pretend to be greener than they actually are. They often support organisations while at the core they are still very polluting. We chose LEGO, which has its own sustainability programme, and Cartoon Network, which launched a platform about climate for young people. But we also set up a collaboration with the US Department of State and the Department of Education in New York and LA.

On the other hand, I got in touch with Mark Lens, a successful entrepreneur, who just then had decided to set up his own non-profit organisation Ondernemers voor Warm België. His organisation covers a multitude of initiatives: tree planting, giving laptops to the underprivileged, filling empty sandwich boxes, and so on. He is the first person willing to support Project Kakuma on a monthly basis with an amount that has allowed us to keep the project running for two years now and to bear unforeseen costs: a fence that is broken, a cupboard to store the laptops …

To be able to create top-down impact and grow further, we launched a new programme in 2022, inspired by surveys which showed that teachers saw two main opportunities. On the one hand, teachers want to be trained and receive certificates. On the other hand, they think a six-week project is too short. That's why we developed the Climate Action Schools. A programme spread out over a full academic year, in which we want to involve the whole school and also provide in-service training for teachers. Today almost every school has an ICT coordinator in charge of technology and computers on a school campus. We created a new role: the Climate Champion. This person is responsible for sustainability in the school and guides all teachers in implementing climate education in the school. Although the programme is not free, we always ensure that half of the participating schools are sponsored. This allows schools that lack financial resources to participate as well. Especially for this programme, we developed a platform that is a mix of social media and an electronic learning environment. After all, we noticed that existing learning environments such as Blackboard, Canvas and Moodle are too focused on content and examination. With our new platform, we want to put networking and learning at the centre. In the platform, teachers can write public messages, ask for help, chat, create and share lessons and stories, build a network, create groups and surround themselves with teachers who want to work on the same project, or plan a virtual interaction. They can build their own profile and search specifically for other teachers in certain countries, within a particular subject area, with a certain expertise or on the basis of shared interests. But we also added new features that meet with great enthusiasm from users. For instance, they can visualise their network with an interactive print. In addition, all virtual interactions between classes can be shown on a world map. A digital alternative to the world map with pins hanging at the back wall in some classrooms.

Meanwhile, TAG is a thriving non-profit organization with various initiatives and a large team. Jennifer in the US is working with Riley, Dave, Justin, Al, Ateken, Lindsay, Hope and Scott. In Belgium, where I am based, we can count on Bram, Wout and Nine. The rest of our team is spread all over the world: Hila in Singapore, Maria in Peru, Carla in Switzerland, Yiting in China, Riya and Catherine in Canada, Ayanfe in Rwanda, Rachael in Jamaica, Tam in Vietnam and, of course, Franco, William and Simon in Kakuma. Jennifer and I meet via Zoom daily and are continuously exchanging ideas and insights via Telegram. There is a six-hour time difference that makes collaboration not evident. But that also ensures that the TAG team is constantly active. We meet only once a year, yet everything goes smoothly. To be director of a large NGO, you definitely need to have a growth mindset. Every day,

I proudly have conversations in English with experts and large organisations. And with our team. But in the morning I never dread going to work.

With Dr Jennifer Williams

15 FUTURE

I look into Mustafa's eyes as a pain shoots through my left shoulder. This does not feel good. The Swede has just pulled my arm, dislocating it. The doctor rushes to me and runs some tests. His verdict is merciless: this camp is over. But I tell him that I have been looking forward to this for too long and ask him to tape up my left arm. I continue with one arm. After a moment's hesitation, he agrees, and I can continue my camp against the Swede. No less than ten years I have been training in the national team for this moment. One minute to go. I miss Mustafa narrowly and then I dislocate my arm for a second time. My European championship is over. It would later turn out that my shoulder could no longer handle top-class sport. When I was twenty, my trainer Maurizio stated that I am a late bloomer. I would only be ready to reach finals at European and world championships around the age of 25. And he was right. In Lithuania, I won bronze at 26. But in Portugal, my karate career will turn out to be over. Which had actually yet to begin. Earlier, the world championships in Japan were cancelled due to swine flu. Double bad luck. Deep disappointment followed this championship. You could say I failed. After a decade of training up to five times a week and denying myself almost everything, I had to throw in the towel just before the climax was due. Now I look at it differently and realise that the same thing happened with the Kakuma project. In both my sports career and the project, there were often hopeless moments. A growth mindset was totally unknown to me

European championships karate

at that time. Quitting would surely have left me with a sour feeling, should I now look back on the results. Now I look back on only small successes.

The same thing happened in 2019 when I was asked to speak at the European Parliament. A great opportunity for which I wanted to prepare thoroughly. In my case, that means working on a script for days and a spending at least half a day on each slide of my presentation. When the moment came, I lost my voice. At such times, it's just about how you deal with setbacks. Keep seizing opportunities and lift yourself to the next level.

How do you want to be remembered by future generations? Will you succeed in leaving something lasting behind to the world? Something that future generations will still talk about? Will it be a book or a song that your grandchildren will be proud of to talk about? Perhaps an invention? Or rather a domain name that they will make handy use of? Possibly even a business or initiative they will gratefully pursue. Let's hope it's a stamp that contributes to the lives of your progeny. Because the back of this stamp is certainly a huge ecological footprint that has left lasting damage.

My Australian friend Ken Silburn once said that helping people is addictive. He is right. Whether you start a small initiative or a full-blown movement, you will always bump into walls. But if you persevere at crucial moments, extraordinary things happen.

Meanwhile, TAG has come of age. In 2022, we received accreditation from the United Nations Environmental Program (UNEP). In 2023, the Climate Action Project was named one of the ten Education 4.0 lighthouses of the World Economic Forum (WEF). In addition, we are now part of UNESCO's Teacher Task Force. Others who have received this honour include ministries of education in several countries and large organisations such as Microsoft and LEGO Foundation. For the first time, we are not working purely bottom-up, but also top-down. Now that - including with TAG - we are also supported by governments, the potential to reach more teachers and students is much higher. In the Philippines, for instance, there are as many as 28 million pupils. My goal in my lifetime is to have reached one billion learners with one of my initiatives, enriching and hopefully even improving their lives.

I have always followed one rule: when I support an initiative financially, it must help an entire community. I get requests to help people almost daily, but I have started to realise that unfortunately you cannot help everyone. Still, there are inspiring initiatives I am involved in. Together with Kaossara Sani, I am working on a borehole in Togo so that an entire community has clean water. I also sent two drones to Andrews in Malawi so that he can get a better view of his large-scale tree planting.

As I drove through Kakuma, I noticed plastic being burnt on every corner. Even in a school in Nairobi, there was a place where waste was constantly being burnt. The air pollution associated with this is significant. What if we could not only eliminate this pollution, but also use the waste as raw material for new materials? Materials that may not even be in stock. Together with Hasselt University, I have developed a plastic machine, which first converts plastic waste into small flakes that can then be used to develop new materials by injecting liquid plastic into a mould. We will send this machine to the Kakuma Refugee Camp. The fantastic thing about this story is that it comes full circle: the raw material is free, but you can use it to develop new resources that you can sell for very small amounts. If you were to give them away for free, you get no appreciation and the item might still end up on the roadside somewhere. So only financial support is needed to develop the plastic machines. And with the proceeds, the people doing the work can be compensated. As a bonus, we could make wristbands there, from recycled plastic, so that people also get an affinity with the product. The fact that this project brings sustainability and refugees together is a very big bonus.

In Kakuma, everything is going according to plan. Our consultant Nhial is now studying at a prestigious university and spoke at the UN about refugee life and the importance of education. He recently met Britain's Prince Harry. While I can only be proud of Nhial, there is also something unfortunate about this. Brain drain is a universal fact: the greatest talents migrate to other places, so you have to provide for succession. Fortunately, some people come back to give something back. For instance, there is Josef who got out of the camp and is taking classes at Harvard. He decided to set up a project on programming in the camp and is using our infrastructure to do so. It is fantastic to see how fifty young people who have never seen a laptop before can create a simple website after just one month. It inspires Franco and me to set up similar projects: graphic design, Scratch, and so on. Each time, our initiatives can count on the interest of many young people who never used a computer before, but can design the most beautiful things in a short time. These young people always participate in the Climate Action Project too. They planted trees, recycled plastic bottles and built a solar-powered fan. During Climate Action Day, they asked questions to President Michel of Seychelles and presented their work to hundreds of thousands of people. We now teach sign language classes in Kakuma and train teachers. What started with a simple idea has grown into an inspiring place where young people can get opportunities and discover their potential.

Franco sends me a video of a deaf-mute girl using sign language to explain her solution to climate change. After a few minutes, she receives applause from her peers. And that is special, because until recently, young people with hearing impairments had a pretty hard time in the camp. They are often excluded. It touches me that this girl is allowed to receive appreciation.

Perseverance can sideline talent. I have ceased my search for the next Einstein in Africa. Every human being has enormous potential. What is much more important is the right mindset. An Indian student who participated in the Climate Action Project stated, 'Climate is changing, why aren't we?' You too have the potential to make a positive impact. To do something great. What ... I'll let you fill in the blanks! You decide how many people can be touched by this.

The sky is the limit, some say, but that is not actually true. When Rick from NASA once suggested to me to send drawings and messages from our participants to Mars, it became clear to me that the limit is beyond our sky.

As I open WhatsApp, I notice a message from Franco. He has been working for me at Kakuma Refugee Camp for four years, even before we had our own school there. Darn. He tells me that today's lesson with the Irish students was cancelled due to a misunderstanding. And that he therefore decided to play a video so that the students in Kakuma didn't come to our school for nothing. His exact words: 'some motivation videos', accompanied by a nice picture. Lots of children in colourful uniforms watching our television. I zoom in on the picture and see Mr Bean.

What an unforgettable, educational highlight those students had. Satisfied and with a broad smile, I close the post. I share the fun anecdote with our community.

Today is a good day!

FUTURE

Learning from Mr Bean at our school in Kakuma

Watch my TEDx Talk and learn more about the rationale behind the Kakuma Project and the Climate Action Project.

AFTERWORD

Princess Esmeralda of Belgium

"Education is the most powerful weapon you can use to change the world."

Nelson Mandela

There is no doubt that education can transform a person's life. It provides opportunities and can open the way to a job and a better life. Particularly education for girls is often the key to preventing child marriages and pregnancies at an early age and controlling overpopulation. As an African proverb states: 'If you can educate a girl, you educate a nation'. Because women not only improve living standards for themselves, but also for their families and communities.

Millions of success stories worldwide have been made possible thanks to education. A few years ago, I met a woman whose entire life had changed and who would create impact herself. Neema Namadamu is an inspiration to many in her country. She was born in a small village in the mountains of South Kivu in the Democratic Republic of Congo. A place plagued by violence, mostly gender-based, insecurity, malnutrition, disease and poverty. When she turned two, she contracted polio, which left her disabled. Her father left her family declaring that his daughter was 'a lost cause' because no one would ever marry her. Unfortunately, women in that continent can only survive if they marry, otherwise they are not allowed to own or inherit anything. But Neema's mother, who was alphabetical, believed education could save her. Since the family could not afford crutches, she carried her daughter to school on her back. Surely a distance of several kilometres. When Neema was older and her mother could no longer carry her, she stayed with her uncle in the countryside. When she finished school, she was the first disabled woman in her community to get a university degree. She learnt six languages, worked in parliament and became an advisor to the Ministry of Gender, Family and the Child, where she dedicated herself to supporting women with disabilities. She then decided to help girls in remote villages by letting them go to school. She also fought against

Princess Esmeralda of Belgium and Koen, listening to Greta Thunberg in NYC, 2019

the stigma of menstruation that often caused girls to miss classes due to lack of sanitary pads or even drop out of school.

Today, Neema is an international speaker for women's rights in her country and for nature. She spoke in front of large audiences in the US, was received at the White House and she won countless awards. She started several projects to support women, teach them digital skills and also let them share their stories. For another project, she planted 70 000 trees near villages, aiming to fight deforestation and educate local communities about the ecological crisis.

'I am a real poster girl for the promotion of education,' she keeps saying, adding, 'I am aware that I was lucky to get polio, become crippled, that I was unable to marry and unable to carry water.' A role assigned to so many women in this patriarchal society. This is the paradigm through which she wants to change eastern Congo.

Education is also essential to combat climate change. It can accelerate the development of new technologies. More so, according to a recent study, investing in education can reduce vulnerability. Citizens who were educated are less vulnerable to the impacts of climate change, argues a study published in *Nature Sustainability*. Educated people are less vulnerable to the effects of the climate crisis because it changes their behaviour. For example, how they consume. They adopt sustainable patterns and become aware of risks. And above all, they gain environmental awareness. We need to give children every opportunity so that they can better understand today's biggest problems. We need to empower them and make them custodians of our planet. Climate education should become a compulsory subject in every country.

Koen Timmers has been a pioneer, ensuring that teachers teach about climate change. With his Climate Action Project, he connects millions of children worldwide and ensures they understand the causes and the impact of climate change. And that they come up with solutions. The results were inspiring, creative and captured the imagination.

During the past few years, young people took to the streets to express their fear for the future. They want quick action, believe in science and want to learn. Let us help them change the world.

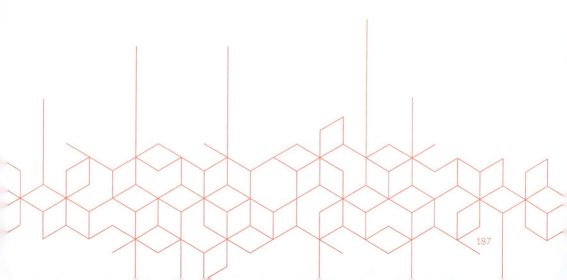

REFERENCES

- Anderson, T. & Dron, J. (2014). *Teaching Crowds: Learning and Social Media*. Unpublished, 101.
- Anderson, V., & Johnson, L. (1997). Systems thinking basics. *Pegasus Communications*, 1-14.
- Andreas, S. (2018). Strong Performers and Successful Reformers in Education World Class. *How to Build a 21st-Century School System*. OECD Publishing.
- Bandura, A. (1989). Regulation of cognitive processes through perceived selfefficacy. *Developmental psychology, 25*(5), 729.
- Bhowmik, A. K., McCaffrey, M. S., Ruskey, A. M., Frischmann, C., & Gaffney, O. (2020). Powers of 10: seeking 'sweet spots' for rapid climate and sustainability actions between individual and global scales. *Environmental Research Letters, 15*(9), 094011.
- Bleijenberg, C., Renes, R.J., Aarts, N., Moons, J. (2020). Het spel en de knikkers: ervaren rechtvaardigheid in vier lokale participatieprocessen. *Bestuurswetenschappen, 74*(2), 51-67.
- Boudet, H., Ardoin, N. M., Flora, J., Armel, K. C., Desai, M., & Robinson, T. N. (2016). Effects of a behaviour change intervention for Girl Scouts on child and parent energy-saving behaviours. *Nature Energy, 1*(8), 1-10.
- Brause, R. S., & Mayher, J. S. (Eds.). (1991). *Search and re-search: What the inquiring teacher needs to know* (Vol. 2). Psychology Press.
- Brown, J.S. & Duguid, P. (2000). *The Social Life of Information*, Harvard Business School Press.
- Bouman, T., Verschoor, M., Albers, C. J., Böhm, G., Fisherd, S. D., Poortinga, P., Whitmarsh, L., Steg, L. (2020). When worry about climate change leads to climate action: How values, worry and personal responsibility relate to various climate actions. *Global Environmental Change, 62*, 102061.
- Christensen, C. M. (2013). *The innovator's dilemma: when new technologies cause great firms to fail*. Harvard Business Review Press.
- Cialdini, R.B. (2007). Descriptive social norms as underappreciated sources of social control. *Psychometrika, 72*(2), 263.
- Coertjens, L., Boeve-de Pauw, J., De Maeyer, S., & Van Petegem, P. (2010). Do schools make a difference in their students' environmental attitudes and awareness? Evidence from PISA 2006. *International Journal of Science and Mathematics Education, 8*(3), 497-522.

- Coward, R. (1990). Greening the child. *New Statesman and Society*, 3, 40-41. May.
- Daniel, D. B. (2012). *Promising principles: Translating the science of learning to educational practice*. Journal of Applied Research in Memory and Cognition, 1(4), 251–253.
- De Waal, F. B. (2012). The antiquity of empathy. *Science, 336*(6083), 874-876.
- Deci, E. L., & Ryan, R. M. (2012). Self-determination theory. *Handbook of theories of social psychology, 1*(20), 416-436.
- Deming, W. E., & Edwards, D. W. (1982). *Quality, productivity, and competitive position* (Vol. 183). Massachusetts Institute of Technology, Center for Advanced Engineering Study, Cambridge, MA.
- Devaney, E., O'Brien, M. U., Resnik, H., Keister, S., & Weissberg, R. P. (2006). *Sustainable Schoolwide Social and Emotional Learning (SEL): Implementation Guide and Toolkit*. Collaborative for Academic, Social, and Emotional Learning (NJ3).
- Dillenbourg, P. (1999). *What do you mean by collaborative learning? Collaborative-learning: Cognitive and Computational Approaches*. Oxford, Elsevier, 1-19.
- Dolan, A. M. (2020). *Powerful primary geography: A toolkit for 21st-century learning*. Routledge.
- Dolan, A. M. (Ed.). (2021). *Teaching Climate Change in Primary Schools: An Interdisciplinary Approach*. Routledge.
- Doucet, A., Netolicky, D., Timmers, K., & Tuscano, F. J. (2020). *Thinking About Pedagogy in an Unfolding Pandemic: An independent report on approaches to distance learning during COVID19 school closures* (retrieved from https://issuu.com/educationinternational/docs/2020_research_covid-19_eng).
- Downes, S. (2008). Places to go: Connectivism & connective knowledge. *Innovate: Journal of Online Education, 5*(1), 6.
- DuFour, R. (2004). What is a 'professional learning community'?. Educational leadership, *61*(8), 6-11.
- Dweck, C. S. (2008). *Mindset: The new psychology of success*. Random House Digital, Inc.
- Elwick, A., Burnard, P., Osgood, J., Huhtinen-Hildén, L., & Pitt, J. (2020). Young children's experiences of music and soundings in museum spaces: lessons, trends and turns from the literature. *Journal of Early Childhood Research, 18*(2), 174-188.

- Fabola, A., & Miller, A. (2016, June). *Virtual reality for early education: A study.* In *International Conference on Immersive Learning.* Springer, Cham, 59-72.
- Fien, J. (1993). *Education For the Environment: Critical Curriculum Theorising and Environmental Education.* Geelong: Deakin University Press.
- Fogg, B. J. (2002). *Persuasieve technologie: computers gebruiken om te veranderen wat we denken en doen.* Morgan Kaufmann.
- Ganz, M. (2010). Leading change: Leadership, organization, and social movements. In N. Nohria & R. Khurana, *Handbook of Leadership Theory and Practice.* Danvers, Harvard Business School Press, 1-10.
- Gee, J. P. (2011). Reflections on empirical evidence on games and learning. *Computer games and instruction,* 223232.
- Gert, B. (1967). Hobbes and psychological egoism. *Journal of the History of Ideas, 28*(4), 503-520.
- Gillingham, K., & Stock, J. H. (2018). The cost of reducing greenhouse gas emissions. *Journal of Economic Perspectives, 32*(4), 53-72.
- Godin, S., & Gladwell, M. (2001). *Unleashing the Ideavirus: Stop Marketing AT People! Turn Your Ideas into Epidemics by Helping Your Customers Do the Marketing Thing for You.* Hachette Books.
- Greenberg, M. T., Weissberg, R. P., O'Brien, M. U., Zins, J. E., Fredericks, L., Resnik, H., & Elias, M. J. (2003). Enhancing school-based prevention and youth development through coordinated social, emotional, and academic learning. *American psychologist, 58*(6-7), 466.
- Gupta, S., Tirpak,D. A., Burger, N., Gupta, J., Höhne, N., Boncheva, A. I., Kanoan, G. M., Kolstad, C., Kruger, J.A., Michaelowa, A., Murase, S., Pershing, J., Saijo, T. & Sari, A. (2007). Policies, Instruments and Co-operative Arrangements. In B. Metz, O.R. Davidson, P.R. Bosch, R. Dave, L.A. Meyer (eds.). *Climate Change 2007: Mitigation. Contribution of Working Group III to the Fourth Assessment Report of the Intergovernmental Panel on Climate Change.* Cambridge University Press, Cambridge, UK and New York, NY, USA.
- Haenlein, M., & Kaplan, A. (2019). A brief history of artificial intelligence: On the past, present, and future of artificial intelligence. *California management review, 61*(4), 5-14.
- Halvorsen, A. L., Duke, N. K., Brugar, K. A., Block, M. K., Strachan, S. L., Berka, M. B., & Brown, J. M. (2012). Narrowing the achievement gap in second-grade social studies and content area literacy: The promise of a project-based approach. *Theory & Research in Social Education, 40*(3), 198-229.

- Hammond, Z. (2014). *Culturally responsive teaching and the brain: Promoting authentic engagement and rigor among culturally and linguistically diverse students*. Corwin Press.
- Harari, Y. N. (2014). *Sapiens: A brief history of humankind*. Random House.
- Hsu, A., & Zomer, A. (2014). *Environmental performance index*. Wiley StatsRef: Statistics Reference Online, 1-5.
- Immordino-Yang, M. H., & Damasio, A. (2007). We feel, therefore we learn: The relevance of affective and social neuroscience to education. *Mind, brain, and education, 1*(1), 3-10.
- Jutten, J., & Leren, S. D. (2010). *Systeemdenken in de klas*. Uitgeverij Betelgeuze.
- Kaner, S. (2014). *Facilitator's guide to participatory decision-making*. John Wiley & Sons.
- Kelleher, I., & Whitman, G. (2018). A bridge no longer too far: A case study of one school's exploration of the promise and possibilities of mind, brain, and education science for the future of education. *Mind, Brain, and Education, 12*(4), 224-230.
- Kidd, C., Piantadosi, S. T., & Aslin, R. N. (2012). The Goldilocks effect: Human infants allocate attention to visual sequences that are neither too simple nor too complex. *PloS one, 7*(5), e36399.
- Koehler, M., & Mishra, P. (2009). *What is technological pedagogical content knowledge (TPACK)?*. Contemporary issues in technology and teacher education, 9(1), 60-70.
- Kruse, S. D., Louis, K. S., & Bryk, A. (1995). An emerging framework for analyzing school-based professional community. In K. S. Louis & S. D. Kruse (Eds.), *Professionalism and community: Perspectives on reforming urban schools*. Thousand Oaks, CA, USA?
- Krznaric, R. (2020*). The good ancestor: how to think long term in a short-term world*. Random House.
- Kuhn, D., Zillmer, N., Crowell, A., & Zavala, J. (2013). Developing norms of argumentation: Metacognitive, espistemological, and social dimensions of developing argumentive competence. *Cognition & Instruction, 31*, 456-496.
- Kurzweil, R. (2005). *The singularity is near: When humans transcend biology*. Penguin.
- Kwauk, C. (2020). *Roadblocks to Quality Education in a Time of Climate Change*. Brief. Center for Universal Education at The Brookings Institution.

- Ladson-Billings, G. (1995). Toward a theory of culturally relevant pedagogy. *American educational research journal, 32*(3), 465-491.
- Larmer, J., & Mergendoller, J. R. (2010). Seven essentials for project-based learning. *Educational leadership, 68*(1), 34-37.
- Latour, B. (1996). *On actor-network theory: A few clarifications.* Soziale welt, 369-381.
- Lave, J., Resnick, L. B. & Levine, J. M. (Eds.) (1991). Situating learning in communities of practice. *Perspectives on socially shared cognition, xiii. Perspectives on socially shared cognition,* Washington DC, USA, 63-82.
- Lave, J. (1996). Teaching, as learning, in practice. *Mind, culture, and activity, 3*(3), 149-164.
- Lawson, D. F., Stevenson, K. T., Peterson, M. N., Carrier, S. J., Strnad, R. L., & Seekamp, E. (2019). Children can foster climate change concern among their parents. *Nature Climate Change, 9*(6), 458-462.
- Lawson, D. F., Stevenson, K. T., Peterson, M. N., Carrier, S. J., Strnad, R., & Seekamp, E. (2018). Intergenerational learning: are children key in spurring climate action? *Global Environmental Change, 53,* 204-208.
- Liu, L., Du, X., Zhang, Z., & Zhou, J. (2019). Effect of problem-based learning in pharmacology education: A meta-analysis. *Studies in Educational Evaluation, 60,* 43-58.
- McCright, A. M., & Dunlap, R. E. (2011). The politicization of climate change and polarization in the American public's views of global warming, 2001–2010. *The Sociological Quarterly, 52*(2), 155-194.
- McGee, P. Deeper (2006). *Learning Through a Contribution Model for Learning Object Design.* 29th annual, 302.
- Michie, S., Atkins, L., West. R., Goosen. H., van't Hof, K., & Mehra. S. (2018). *Het gedragsveranderingswiel: 8 stappen naar succesvolle interventies.* Amsterdam University Press.
- Minocha, S., Tilling, S. & Tudor, A.-D. (2018). Role of Virtual Reality in Geography and Science Fieldwork Education. In: *Knowledge Exchange Seminar Series, Learning from New Technology.* 25 Apr 2018, Belfast.
- Miyashiro, M. R., & Colonna, J. (2011). *The empathy factor: Your competitive advantage for personal, team, and business success.* PuddleDancer Press.
- Murdoch, K. (2010). *An overview of the Integrated Inquiry planning model.* Retrieved from http://static1.squarespace.com/static/55c7efeae4b0f5d2463be2d1/t/55ca9b43e4b0cf5cb3c4baa5/1439341379536/murdochmodelforinquiry2010.pdf

- O'Brien, K., & Sygna, L. (2013). *Responding to climate change: the three spheres of transformation. Proceedings of transformation in a changing climate, 16*, 23.
- Pearlman, B. (2009). Making 21st century schools: Creating learner-centered schoolplaces/workplaces for a new culture of students at work. *Educational Technology*, 14-19.
- Piaget, J. (1976). Piaget's Theory. In: B. Inhelder, H. H. Chipman & C. Zwingmann (eds.), *Piaget and His School*. Springer Study Edition. Springer, Berlin, Heidelberg.
- Piaget, J (1959). *The Early Growth of Logic in the Child: Classification and Seriation*.
- Pijanowski, L. (2008). Striking a balance. *The Learning Professional, 29*(4), 43.
- Pörtner, H. O., Roberts, D. C., Poloczanska, E. S., Mintenbeck, K., Tignor, M., Alegría, A., ... & Okem, A. (2022). *IPCC, 2022: Summary for policymakers*.
- Puentedura, R. (2006). *Transformation, technology, and education* [Blog post].
- Rogers, E. M. (1995). *Diffusion of Innovations: modifications of a model for telecommunications. In Die Diffusion von Innovationen in der Telekommunikation.* Springer, 25-38.
- Saavedra, A. R., Liu, Y., Haderlein, S. K., Rapaport, A., Garland, M., Hoepfner, D., ... & Hu, A. (2021). *Knowledge in Action Efficacy Study Over Two Years*. Online Submission, 2021 ERIC, https://eric.ed.gov/?id=ED616435
- Samaddar, S., Chatterjee, R., Misra, B., & Tatano, H. (2014). Outcome-expectancy and self-efficacy: reasons or results of flood preparedness intention? *International journal of disaster risk reduction, 8*, 91-99.
- Savery, J. R. (2015). Overview of problem-based learning: Definitions and distinctions. *Essential readings in problem-based learning: Exploring and extending the legacy of Howard S. Barrows, 9*, Purdue University Press, 5-15. https://doi.org/10.2307/j.ctt6wq6fh
- Schleicher, A. (2011). The case for 21st century learning. *OECD Observer, 282*(283), 42-43.
- Schleicher, A. (2019). *PISA 2018: Insights and Interpretations*. OECD Publishing.
- Schwab, K. (2017). *The fourth industrial revolution*. Currency.
- Senge, P. M., Cambron-McCabe, N., Lucas, T., Smith, B., & Dutton, J. (2012). *Schools that learn (updated and revised): A fifth discipline fieldbook for educators, parents, and everyone who cares about education*. Currency.
- Shadiev, R., Hwang, W. Y., Huang, Y. M., & Liu, T. Y. (2018). Facilitating application of language skills in authentic environments with a mobile learning system. *Journal of Computer Assisted Learning, 34*(1), 42-52.

- Shear, L., Tan, C. K., Patel, D., Trinidad, G., Koh, R., & Png, S. (2014). ICT and Instructional Innovation: The Case of Crescent Girls' School in Singapore. *International Journal of Education and Development using Information and Communication Technology, 10*(2), 77-88.
- Siemens, G. (2008). Learning and knowing in networks: Changing roles for educators and designers. *ITFORUM for Discussion, 27*(1), 1-26.
- Simons, R. J., Van der Linden, J., & Duffy, T. (2000). *New learning: Three ways to learn in a new balance.* In New learning. Springer, 1-20.
- Skinner, B. F. (1963). Behaviorism at fifty. *Science, 140*(3570), 951-958.
- Smith, K. A., Sheppard, S. D., Johnson, D. W., & Johnson, R. T. (2005). Pedagogies of engagement: Classroom-based practices. *Journal of Engineering Education, 94*(1), 87-101.
- Smolen, P., Zhang, Y., & Byrne, J. H. (2016). The right time to learn: mechanisms and optimization of spaced learning. *Nature Reviews Neuroscience, 17*(2), 77.
- Spence, A., Poortinga, W., & Pidgeon, N. (2012). The psychological distance of climate change. *Risk Analysis: An International Journal, 32*(6), 957-972
- Spencer, J. (2016). The Difference Between Cooperation and Collaboration. Retrieved from https://spencerauthor.com/can-you-force-collaboration/
- Steg, L., Perlaviciute, G., & van der Werff, E. (2015). Understanding the human dimensions of a sustainable energy transition. *Frontiers in psychology, 6*, 805.
- Stern, P. C. (2000). Toward a Coherent Theory of Environmentally Significant Behavior. *Journal of Social Issues, 56*(3), 407-424.
- Strong, R. (1995). What Do Students Want? *Educational leadership, 53*(1), 8-12.
- Struyven, K. (2009). Activerende werkvormen beter dan hoorcolleges? *Caleidoscoop, 21*(5), 18-21.
- Struyven, K., Dochy, F., & Janssens, S. (2008). Students' likes and dislikes regarding student-activating and lecture-based educational settings: Consequences for students' perceptions of the learning environment, student learning and performance. *European Journal of Psychology of Education, 23*(3), 295-317.
- Surma, T., Vanhoyweghen, K., Sluijsmans, D., Camp, G., Muijs, D., & Kirschner, P. A. (2019). *Wijze lessen: twaalf bouwstenen voor effectieve didactiek.* Ten Brink Uitgevers.
- Sweller, J. (2011). Cognitive load theory. *Psychology of learning and motivation,* Vol. 55, 37-76. Academic Press.
- Thaler, R. H. & Sunstein, C. S. (2008). *Nudge: Improving decisions about health, wealth, and happiness.* Yale University Press.

- Thomas, L. (2017). *Are parents being heard? Parents' experiences of participating in multi-professional meetings as part of the Education, Health and Care Plan process* (Doctoral dissertation, University of Birmingham).
- Tilbury, D. (1992). Environmental education: A head, heart and hand approach to learning about environmental problems. *Education, 7*.
- Timmers, K. (2018). Evolution of technology in the classroom. *In Teaching in the Fourth Industrial Revolution*. Routledge, 106-123.
- Tinto, V. (1998). Colleges as communities: Taking research on student persistence seriously. *The Review of Higher Education, 21*(2), 167-177
- Trinomics, and ICF (2018). *Impacts of circular economy policies on the labour market. Final report*. https://circulareconomy. europa. eu/platform/sites/default/files/ec_2018_-_impacts_of_circular_economy_policies_on_the_labour_market. pdf [10 July 2020].
- Trope, Y., & Liberman, N. (2010). Construal-level theory of psychological distance. *Psychological review, 117*(2), 440.
- Van den Branden, K. (2015). *Onderwijs voor de 21ste eeuw*. ACCO, 256.
- van Gennip, H., Marx, T., & Smeets, E. (2006). *Ontwikkeling instrument didactisch handelen*. Vier In Balans Monitor. ITS https://www.researchgate.net/publication/265232336_Ontwikkeling_instrument_didactisch_handelen_Vier_In_Balans_Monitor_Pilotstudie
- Vega, V., & Terada, Y. (2012). *Research supports collaborative learning*. Edutopia, http://www.edutopia.org/stw-collaborative-learning-research
- Verplanken, B., & Roy, D. (2016). Empowering interventions to promote sustainable lifestyles: Testing the habit discontinuity hypothesis in a field experiment. *Journal of Environmental Psychology, 45*, 127-134.
- Verschoor, J. (2020). *EPiC Series in Education Science. Proceedings of the MIT LINC, 3*, 251-257.
- Vygotski, L. S., & Cole, M. (1978). *Mind in society: Development of higher psychological processes*. Harvard university press.
- Watson, J. B. (1957). *Behaviorism* (Vol. 23). Transaction Publishers.
- Weiss, C. (1995). The four 'I's' of school reform: How interests, ideology, information, and institution affect teachers and principals. *Harvard educational review, 65*(4), 571-593.
- Wenger, E. (1998). Communities of practice: Learning as a social system. *Systems thinker, 9*(5), 2-3.
- Wojcicki, E. (2019). *How to Raise Successful People: Simple Lessons for Radical Results*. Houghton Mifflin Harcourt.

- Wolpert-Gawron, H. (2016). *What the heck is inquiry-based learning?* https://www.edutopia.org/blog/what-heck-inquiry-based-learning-heather-wolpert-gawron
- Zaval, L., Markowitz, E. M., & Weber, E. U. (2015). How will I be remembered? Conserving the environment for the sake of one's legacy. *Psychological science, 26*(2), 231-236.

Websites

- Ashoka. (2021, April 18). Welcome to Ashoka's Systems Change Crash Course. http://ashoka.org/en-us/program/systems-change-crash-course
- Climate Visuals. (2021, May 27) 7 core principles for climate change communication. http://climatevisuals.org/evidence
- Cornell University, Center for Teaching Innovation. (2021, September 28). Collaborative Learning. https://teaching.cornell.edu/teaching-resources/active-collaborative-learning/collaborative-learning
- Educause. (2021, May 26). 2021 EDUCAUSE Horizon Report® | Teaching and Learning Edition. http://library.educause.edu/resources/2021/4/2021-educause-horizon-report-teaching-and-learning-edition
- Gapminder. (2016, March 29). Dollar street. http://gapminder.org/dollar-street
- McKinsey & Company. (2018, October 27). Jobs lost, jobs gained: What the future of work will mean for jobs, skills, and wages. http://mckinsey.com/featured-insights/future-of-work/jobs-lost-jobs-gained-what-the-future-of-work-will-mean-for-jobs-skills-and-wages
- Project Drawdown. (2020, April 4). Table of solutions. http://drawdown.org/solutions/table-of-solutions
- TED (2014, April 17). Hans Rosling. http://ted.com/speakers/hans_rosling
- TED. (2014, April 15). Paper beats plastic? How to rethink environmental folklore. http://ted.com/talks/leyla_acaroglu_paper_beats_plastic_how_to_rethink_environmental_folklore
- TED. (2022, January 7). The One Thing All Great Teachers Do. https://www.ted.com/talks/nick_fuhrman_the_one_thing_all_great_teachers_do
- TED. (2023, April 7). Grit: The power of passion and perseverance. http://ted.com/talks/angela_lee_duckworth_grit_the_power_of_passion_and_perseverance

- TED. (2023, May 2). How great leaders inspire action. http://ted.com/talks/simon_sinek_how_great_leaders_inspire_action?language=en
- TED. (2023, May 29). 3 strategies for effectively talking about climate change. http://ted.com/talks/john_marshall_3_strategies_for_effectively_talking_about_climate_change
- The British Psychological Society. (2020, January 20). Meta analysis of 64 studies involving 6000 participants finds that self-explanation is a powerful learning technique. http://digest.bps.org.uk/2018/12/07/meta-analysis-of-64-studies-involving-6000-participants-finds-that-self-explanation-is-a-powerful-learning-technique
- UNESCO. (2022, December 13). UNESCO urges making environmental education a core curriculum component in all countries by 2025. http://en.unesco.org/news/unesco-urges-making-environmental-education-core-curriculum-component-all-countries-2025
- UNHCR. (2017, August 30). Education Strategy Kakuma Refugee Camp Kenya. http://data2.unhcr.org/en/documents/download/65138
- UNHCR. (2017, May 16). Kakuma Refugee Camp and Kalobeyei Integrated Settlement. http://unhcr.org/ke/kakuma-refugee-camp
- University of Cambridge. (2021, April 23). Teaching pupils to 'think like Da Vinci' will help them to take on climate change. http://cam.ac.uk/research/news/teaching-pupils-to-think-like-da-vinci-will-help-them-to-take-on-climate-change
- World Economic Forum. (2023, February 17). Education 4.0 Lighthouses. http://initiatives.weforum.org/reskilling-revolution/education-lighthouses